HAVING COFFEE WITH GOD

HAVING COFFEE WITH GOD

Mark Barnette

Advocate Press, Columbia, South Carolina

Copyright © 2024 by Advocate Press

Scripture quotations marked (KJV) are taken from the King James Bible (public domain).

Scripture quotations marked (MSG) are taken from THE MESSAGE, copyright © 1993, 2002, 2018 by Eugene H. Peterson. Used by permission of NavPress. All rights reserved. Represented by Tyndale House Publishers, Inc.

Scripture quotations marked (NIV) are taken from The Holy Bible, New International Version, Copyright © 1973, 1978, 1984 by the International Bible Society. THE HOLY BIBLE, NEW INTERNATIONAL VERSION®, NIV® Copyright © 1973, 1978, 1984, 2011 by Biblica, Inc.® Used by permission. All rights reserved worldwide.

Scripture quotations marked (TLB) are taken from The Living Bible copyright © 1971 by Tyndale House Foundation. Used by permission of Tyndale House Publishers Inc., Carol Stream, Illinois 60188. All rights reserved.

All rights reserved. No part of this book may be reproduced or transmitted in any form or by any means, electronic or mechanical, including photocopying, recording, or by any information storage and retrieval system, without permission in writing from the publisher.

First published in the United States of America in 2024

Library of Congress Cataloging-in-Publication Data
Having Coffee with God
p. cm.

ISBN 978-1-966237-06-8

First, and most important, I would like to dedicate this meager work to God and my Lord and Savior Jesus Christ, who motivated me to record some of our many conversations.

Next, I dedicate this to my wife Elizabeth, who did not turn away from me when I told her of my talking with God but comforted and supported me in my efforts to record the words I heard.

Finally, to Jessica, who has been central to my journey and made this dream come true.

Table of Contents

Foreword ix
Chapter 1: The Beginning of My Journey 1
Chapter 2: The Age of the Prophets 4
Chapter 3: Why Belief Matters 7
Chapter 4: A Chance Conversation 10
Chapter 5: It's Showtime 14
Chapter 6: What Is Truth? 17
Chapter 7: Another Conversation 19
Chapter 8: A Conversation on Purpose 24
Chapter 9: God and the Lottery 27
Chapter 10: A Glass of Water 31
Chapter 11: Thoughts on Consciousness 34
Chapter 12: The Devil Comes at 3:00 a.m. 36
Chapter 13: Knowledge and Wisdom 40
Chapter 14: Cause and Effect 43
Chapter 15: Faith 46
Chapter 16: Having Faith in Your Purpose 50
Chapter 17: Judge Not 53
Chapter 18: God 2.0 59
Chapter 19: Why Is Having Faith So Hard 63
Chapter 20: The Easter Cross at Sunset 67
Chapter 21: What Is Forever? 71
Chapter 22: Why Bad Things Happen 74
Chapter 23: The Bible Is Infallible, Right? 76
Chapter 24: Find Your God Sense 81
Chapter 25: Second Chances 84
Chapter 26: Dichotomy 88
Chapter 27: Be Careful What You Pray For 92
Chapter 28: The Joke Is on Us 95
Chapter 29: What Is Proof? 99
Chapter 30: Endgame 102
Chapter 31: One Final Thought 106
About the Author 109

Foreword

When I was asked by my good friend Mark Barnette to write a foreword for this book, I was immediately excited. Yet writing a foreword raises its own set of questions. Am I signing up to affirm everything that has been written? What if there are theological problems? What if everything is not absolutely correct?

These are just a few of the questions I considered while writing this foreword. First, the title *Having Coffee with God* is ambitious. I think C. S. Lewis is right when he says, "It is safe to tell the pure in heart, they will see God because only the pure in heart want to" (*The Problem of Pain*). In our better moments, we may ask, "Who would not want to have coffee with God?"

Many of us, like Mark, may shy away from such a conversation. He, too, was initially reluctant, only drawn in by the painful loss of a friend and a series of miraculous moments. There's a part of us that may resist having coffee with God, just as Mark did. We may find comfort in the darkness of sin, the power of self-justification, and the worship of ourselves. But this path only leads to despair, as it did in Mark's life, until he accepted the invitation to have coffee with God.

Do not read this book if you are seeking perfect theology; you will not find it. But you will find an experience of a living God who wants to speak into our lives. This is not the gospel according to Mark Barnette, but this is the gospel of the Christ according to Mark

Barnette. I realize the difference is subtle, but it is important. The first could be elitist, but the second is experiential.

This theology is the "Mark-ed up" version of the gospel of the Christ. Mark's purpose is to share an experience of God, who finally got his attention. God speaks. Certainly, the Bible is God's effort to reveal to humanity the need for salvation and God's plan to achieve it.

It culminates in a witness of the living word, Jesus Christ, the Lamb of God, who is sacrificed for our sins and is our savior. This book is Mark's experience of this saving grace and the power of God's mercy for him. The grand narrative of salvation becomes tangible and accessible because God speaks to Mark Barnette.

God speaks also to you. This book has a mission; it is written to bear witness that God wants to make the gospel tangible and accessible to your life. Maybe this book is God's effort to open the conversation with you. The fact that you are even reading this foreword may point to a desire, need, and curiosity to have coffee with God.

Perhaps you have realized the darkness of your broken life, the despair of self-salvation, and the emptiness of self-worship, and you are wondering if God even knows or cares. Mark's experience is a testimony to God's love and care for him but also for everyone who longs to have coffee with God.

Jesus said: "Look at me. I stand at the door. I knock. If you hear me call and open the door, I'll come right in and sit down to supper with you" (Revelation 3:20 MSG).

These words are an invitation to all who are willing to hear and open the door. For Mark, it did not feel like a formal dinner invitation but an opportunity to share a simple cup of coffee to find the love and grace of an eternal friendship. If you hear this knocking, this is an invitation to open the door, just as Mark did.

May you find peace, joy, and hope as you read. Amen.

Reverend Dr. Jon Lovelady, senior pastor
St. John's Presbyterian Church
Jacksonville, Florida

Chapter 1

The Beginning of My Journey

*"Your beginnings will seem humble,
so prosperous will your future be."—Job 8:7 NIV*

First, I should say I have not laid this work out in strictly chronological order of its writing. I struggled with how I might best honor God as I began putting my thoughts on paper. He told me that all those who believe in him will serve him in different ways. Others will glorify God in more dramatic, widely publicized, and certainly more effective ways than I. My calling is softer and quieter, mere words on a page. What follows, then, are in some cases dialogues with God and offered as such. Others are pieces inspired by my conversations with God. In all cases I was moved to write what the Lord has told me. I do this not out of boastfulness or arrogance, but out of humility, amazed that the Lord would use one such as me.

Some will not seem strictly gospel, at least insofar as the organized church is concerned, but what I offer here is a recounting of those moments when God showed me his way. These words, I hope, will help people begin their own journey as they find their own path to the Lord in all his glory.

Second, even in today's unbelievable world, my blessings from God will be doubted by many. They will doubt I have spoken with

God. There will be those who will think I am either delusional or that I have some other, more sinister, motive. None of these are true.

I promise you I am both rational and sane. No one could have been more surprised than I when God blessed me with these words. I accept I am not worthy, but I accept that I am also part of God's plan and always have been, even before I knew it. For those who read and doubt my words, go in peace. I cannot make you believe; that is a choice you must make in your heart.

Finally, for those who read and believe, God will bless your life through your faith. I take no credit for that. I only showed you the door. If you believe, you have opened that door on your own.

We—God and I—discussed how we could use the gift of words he gave me. Playfully, he said I might write a devotional, that I should pick out my favorite 365 Bible verses, and that he would offer me insights to share.

Initially, I thought that sounded like a beautiful idea—and then it occurred to me that to do as he said, I would have to study the Bible to pick out 365 verses. I could feel the Lord's grin. Once again, it confirmed for me that, despite the frowning demeanor of some dour Christians who insist on a stern God, the Lord does have a sense of humor.

Instead, as a beginner, I suggested what was, to my mind, a more straightforward idea. "Why not," I pondered, "jot down our conversations, insights, and my meager reflections on your word."

I immediately realized he already knew my ponderings before my mind could even form the words, and he instantly approved. I sensed this had always been the true intent of God's plans for me.

There were, he shared, already many fine devotionals. What he genuinely wished me to do was document my awareness and growth in my Christian faith. In seeking me out, he wanted me to show a pathway for others who wish to come to Jesus and God. He knew I could not quote scripture, and he knew my mission would not be in preaching to the choir as devotionals usually do. Instead, he wished it to be a beginner's primer on faith. He wished me to show others the first steps on the path to eternity with God. So I metaphorically invited him to sit with me and have a cup of coffee. Therefore, what follows is hopefully just that—at least the conversations, if not the coffee.

To those who read what I have put down, I promise they are the actual, inspired words of God shared with me. I pray you find meaning—and God's love—in these dialogues.

Chapter 2

The Age of the Prophets

"The prophecy of one who hears the words of God, who sees a vision from the Almighty, who falls prostrate, and whose eyes are opened."
—*Numbers 24:4 NIV*

Many people today would say the time of prophecy has passed, that it ended with the coming of the New Testament and the revealing of God's word. They then challenge you to name one recognized prophet since St. John and the book of Revelation. Seriously, I have had those conversations.

Respectfully, God did not go silent with John's passing. He did not "die," though some have proclaimed it so. God has told me something different. He said miracles, prophets, and prophecy continue to this day. If we do not see his works, it is perhaps that we choose not to see them. Regardless, they are all a part of his plan and a way of bringing mankind to him. In fact, for those who seek him, God is revealing his word more openly and broadly than ever before.

While many in the media predict the demise of Christianity, I see things much more hopefully. More and more people are entering into a direct relationship with the Father, and he is freely revealing himself to them. I am certainly not alone in having a relationship with God, nor am I the only one to speak with him. I am sure that if you could get people to be open, you would find an extraordinary number of Christians having a dialogue with God. I can sometimes understand their silence; they fear being thought crazy or dishonest. They would undoubtedly say, "No one talks with God, right? I must either be nuts or a liar."

Not surprisingly, many people—most, in fact—are too embarrassed to admit they are talking with him. Some believe they are imagining things; some are afraid others will think them either mad or demented. And some refuse to listen.

In my case, God answered a simple dare because I initially refused to believe his voice. I thought I was imagining things myself until he performed a little miracle for me. He didn't part the Red Sea or burn a bush, but it was impressive, nonetheless. I will tell you that tale in greater detail in Chapter 4.

That God is speaking to so many people today does not surprise me because—and this is my opinion—we are coming to the end of days. I know this belief has reappeared at various times since the birth and mission of Christ, but I feel moved by the Holy Spirit. While Christ says no one will know the hour of his coming, we do know there will be signs. I believe this to be one of those signs. Truthfully, it does not matter. It is not crucial that I know or can predict the time of the final judgment. It is not my call to make, and it is not a speculation God wishes us to focus on, either.

For those who say I am wrong, and that prophecy is no longer a part of Judeo-Christian tradition, they need look no further than the New Testament: 1 Thessalonians 5:20-21 declares, "Do not treat prophecies with contempt but test them all; hold on to what is good" (NIV).

Also, in Acts 2:17-18 we read that in the last days, God said, "I will pour out my Spirit on all people. Your sons and daughters will prophesy, your young men will see visions, your old men will dream dreams. Even on my servants, both men and women, I will pour out my Spirit in those days, and they will prophesy" (NIV).

Clearly, then, for believers it is still possible. If there is an issue, it is being able to tell a false prophet from a real one, just as it has always been. For that, we must measure the words of the prophecy against God's word as recorded in the Holy Bible.

Any prophecy must confirm God's word and not contradict scripture.

Chapter 3

Why Belief Matters

"Even after Jesus had performed so many signs in their presence, they still would not believe in him."—John 12:37 NIV

I believe in God. And even if I did not, I would still want to believe in him.

Why, you might ask?

Because, aside from any arguments involving religiosity, we need the rules that go with a belief in God, or at least the belief in something greater than ourselves. Without God, life is meaningless.

We cannot hope to survive using a humanist perspective. We desperately need an existence based on something greater than ourselves. One that holds us all to a higher standard and ultimately requires that we account for our actions. Anything humanity can invent, it can destroy, and that includes any society or any culture. History proves this fact time and again.

Some would argue the same statement could also apply to religion, and to some extent, they would be correct, but religions are not God. Religions are manmade conventions that attempt to proscribe how man worships God. It is the failure of moral, fallible humans who too often misunderstand, misconstrue, or misinterpret Jesus. The Son of

God is not responsible for our failings. Rather, he is our salvation from our failings.

Religions have, for centuries, waxed and waned, yet we always come back to a higher being, and I believe that being is the Lord. I believe there is an inherent need for man to believe in something fixed and immutable. Perhaps one could liken it to having a steady point on the horizon to watch when one is in rough seas.

It's a classic argument: moral relativism versus religious moral absolutes. The problem is, and will always be, that for society to exist, we must have absolutes. Murder must always be a crime; theft must always be a crime; rape and incest must always be crimes. Societies have historically held these and other activities as wrong. Religions stand as an impenetrable dam, holding back the flood of human frailty that would overwhelm civilization's incredibly thin veil.

Again, humanists and atheists argue that religion is the real root problem plaguing humanity. There is a knee-jerk reaction among casual observers to condemn Christianity for the many acts of its supposed believers. Christianity—and by that, I mean belief in Jesus Christ—is not to blame for the sins of those who endeavor to live according to Christ's teachings. I would submit that it is not Christianity that is the problem but us. We are the weak link in that chain. We all fall short of the glory of God. Our frailty and imperfection in the face of God's love present the real problem. It is we who are guilty of greed, deceit, murder, and more. We are the ones who misinterpret and corrupt the beautiful spiritual simplicity of God's plan for us. When someone does wrong in the name of Christianity, their actions damn only themselves, not Jesus. God's commandments are clear and unchanging.

Having set forth my brief argument from a philosophical point of view, let me also state a personal vantage point. The reality is simply this: God is as real as the sunrise on a beautiful day. For me, the philosophical argument, while logical, is superfluous. Belief goes beyond subtle points of logic; it stems from faith, and faith comes from understanding the meaning of truth.

My journey toward truth began with my sins of fatalism and arrogance, and it evolved into a conversation and a challenge. Frustrated with my life, I did something foolish. I was stupid enough to dare God. In fact, I double-dog dared him.

Chapter 4

A Chance Conversation

"Do not fear, for I have redeemed you; I have summoned you by name; you are mine."—Isaiah 43:1 NIV

God is a big-picture guy, or at least that is what I had always believed; that was how I saw him. In my mind, the Lord was a distant and disconnected figure, one who neither cared nor concerned himself overly with mankind's daily minutia. I knew such perceptions were not the teachings of Christianity, but my difficult childhood taught me differently.

I thought he had bigger things to worry about than one troubled young boy from a broken home. Though I'd been active in the Christian group Young Life in high school, I admit I was, at best, a mediocre Christian. For much of my life, I gave more attention to my daily comforts than my immortal soul. I long ago accepted the fact that, for me, salvation was both an undeserved and improbable option. For years, I wore that self-imposed death sentence like a badge of honor. I was, I proudly proclaimed, unworthy of salvation.

As an adult, my life became an unmapped journey, and while I accomplished much over the years, things never came into complete focus. I would sometimes wonder why I seemed blessed, but I took it for granted. While I thanked God intermittently, I saw religion as an abstraction, as if philosophical belief alone was sufficient.

This fact also played a role in my years in the spiritual wilderness. I felt God had some plan involving me, but it wasn't something personal to me or one I even particularly wanted. I convinced myself he would understand if I ignored his chosen path for me. While I told myself my faith was important, I also sensed it wasn't important enough. I never inconvenienced myself with the way he laid before me. I had the arrogance over the years to reject his various overtures and faith-based opportunities. They did not appeal to me. So I kept going in a different direction, always believing but from a comfortable distance.

That all changed several years ago when a doctor friend of mine named Howard developed a brain tumor. Although he put on a brave front, we all knew that, medically, his battle was hopeless. As the weeks went by, he grew increasingly feeble.

One morning, as I drove my golf cart with my dog Sailor, I could not stop thinking about Howard. We were in an empty section of our new neighborhood, and there was nothing around me but paved roads and vacant lots.

At that moment, I made what, in hindsight, might be thought a foolish statement. First, I said to God (and certainly not expecting an answer), "Lord, Howard has value in this world, and I am doing nothing of great importance. Take me and not him."

Suddenly and surprisingly, I heard God speaking to me, saying, "You are not offering me anything of value."

I was stunned, partly because of the rebuke but primarily because of the sheer experience of hearing an inner voice—a voice not my own.

"I offered you my life," I replied, both amazed at the sound in my head and somehow offended at the rejected offering.

The direct response stung me. Didn't it say in the Bible something about laying down one's life for one's friends?

"There is a difference," the voice continued, answering my unspoken question. "Jesus spoke about making a sacrifice. You are not making a sacrifice if you give something you deem worthless. In all your years, you have never placed any value on your life, and if you do not, why should I? Do not forget: I know your every thought. I see the intention behind your offer. You are just looking for an easy way out. I have given you a great gift, and you tossed it aside again and again. If you care so little for your life, then it has no worth."

I denied God's response. How dare he attack my motives? How, I thought naively, could he know what I was thinking? I could not conceive that he concerned himself with the needs of each of us. I saw myself as a cog in a larger machine. Any concerns about me, I had always believed, were impersonal. I wasn't a person but a part for him to use or replace if defective.

Instead, I became argumentative.

"That's not true," I challenged God. "I know what it is. You could save him, but you do not. The truth is I've never believed you cared about us individually. You're just a big-picture guy."

Instantly, I followed my challenge with a foolish dare.

"If you care so much," I said, laughing, "let me tell you what I need. I need an O-ring."

In hindsight, it sounds like a silly request, but I was working on a project at home and genuinely needed one.

Moments later, as I approached the next intersection and pulled to a stop, I looked down …

And there on the asphalt directly in front of me lay an O-ring.

I glanced around, nervously. No one was in sight—not a house, not a person, not a car. I was indeed wholly alone.

Feeling rather foolish, I got out of the golf cart and picked the rubber O-ring up.

As I drove the golf cart back home, I defiantly brushed the incident off as nothing more than an incredible coincidence. Hearing nothing but silence, I concluded that God had nothing further to add and that he had made his point—either that, or all that had happened was an incredible example of chaotic convergence. I considered the matter closed, and as I said, I needed the O-ring.

The next day, I was driving with my dog again on the same empty street. Suddenly I realized I was approaching yesterday's intersection. Immediately, my prior conversation came to mind, which I had since written off as a silly daydream.

With an arrogant laugh, I said aloud, "Okay, I'm betting yesterday was a fluke. If you're for real, let me see you do that again."

I approached the same stop sign and looked at the ground before me. Sure enough, there was another O-ring sitting in the road, exactly the same as the first and lying in precisely the same spot.

I stared in stunned disbelief—or should I say belief? I felt humbled, embarrassed, and ashamed.

Yet he offered no rebuke. God was gracious.

I picked up the second O-ring, hurried home, and told my wife the entire story.

Since that day, I have talked to God regularly, and he has shown me so much and guided me toward becoming a better Christian. I will be the first to admit he has had his work cut out for him. I have shared this story many times with many others as a testimony of our living God and his role in our individual lives.

I kept that second O-ring hanging in my home workshop as a reminder.

Then one day, the O-ring suddenly vanished. It was gone from its spot in my workshop, and my wife promised she had not touched it.

After she left the room, I heard God whisper to me, "Now I will teach you the meaning of faith."

Chapter 5

It's Showtime

"Will give our attention to prayer and the ministry of the word."
—Acts 6:4 NIV

The words appeared clearly in my mind. "Your time has come, my son. Are you ready? I will use you for my purpose."

I blinked. "Excuse me—what do you mean my time has come?"

What did God mean? The truth is, I had rejected his call for years—decades—before, and at that time I had, in my mortal human arrogance, refused him. I did not feel worthy. Or perhaps I was too lazy. Regardless, each time previously, I'd answered no.

One of my favorite sayings in my youth was that I accepted my going to hell. Back then, I held no illusions about my future where God was concerned. My sins were too numerous and egregious for me to be worthy of forgiveness. I had figuratively—though not literally—shredded the Ten Commandments, and that's just my Old Testament sins. I had a second complete list for the New Testament. I could not bring myself to forgive myself, and if I could not, I refused to trouble God to do so in my stead. These thoughts were nonsensical at best, sacrilegious at worst, though my mindset was probably somewhere in between.

I had not grasped that granting my own forgiveness was not in my department.

With hindsight, I can say that the Lord has infinite patience.

"I have spent your lifetime waiting for you to come to me." His words were gentle and well-spaced. "I knew you would come. It was a matter of time, and I have all eternity."

"But why wait for me? There are many others, more qualified, more suited, and honestly, more deserving than I?"

"It is not a matter of qualified or deserving, although that might be true, at least as you mean it. But remember Jesus. He is the shepherd gathering his flock. He rescues the sheep that had lost their way. You would certainly qualify on that score."

Was that a sarcastic cheap shot from God, or was he speaking the truth? I tended to go with the latter. It made the most sense.

"You judge yourself too harshly," he added. "In the scheme of eternity, your sins are no worse than any other human. Indeed, that has been true since the beginning. You have free will, that is true, but remember, I can affect changes that direct you if you are the least bit willing."

"I don't understand. If my sins are not a big deal—my words, I know—then why do we have to worry about them at all?"

"A valid question. The answer is subtle but straightforward. As I have said before, it is crucial to be always on guard against Satan's influence, and I emphasize 'at all times.' Humanity believes that Satan tempts explicitly, like a woman seducing you to be unfaithful. I tell you now, Satan's work begins in the mind, not in the deed. It forms in idle thought, evil desire, lust, and greed, to name a few. Look at the Ten Commandments. Everything there begins with a thought. We have talked before on this point. Satan tries to corrupt humanity by any means possible, and the easiest way to corrupt your soul is in your thoughts. That is why it is not enough to not actually commit the sin. Even thinking about it allows Satan to influence you. Things can only get worse from there."

"But how can we stop an idle thought?"

"Being human, you cannot. That is why you must learn to recognize the danger of sinful thoughts, and whenever you commit them, as you no doubt will, ask forgiveness. These are the keys: recognition and seeking forgiveness. This is why Jesus came to you and died for you so that, through him, you will be washed clean of your sins. To achieve forgiveness, one must believe. This is the importance of faith.

"This is the mission I have tasked you with; bring my message of faith and forgiveness to my people. I wish you to help them understand and be vigilant."

Chapter 6

What Is Truth?

"And ye shall know the truth, and the truth shall make you free."
—John 8:32 KJV

Sadly, for many Christians today, truth—like beauty—is in the eye of the beholder. They repeat that verse so much that it has become an almost meaningless cliché. Can everyone have their truth? Is truth fungible? For two people standing together, can it be daytime for one and nighttime for another? Obviously, no. But what then do they mean by that phrase: What is truth?

For one thing, truth is fact, but it is even more fundamental than that. Everyone can have their own opinion or their own experience, but objectively, in the end, there can only be one truth. Like mathematics, it is immutable, which is to say, it is changeless and, therefore, timeless.

Regarding Christianity, people want modern truth to be different from biblical truth. They want it to be something of their own. They want to rationalize their sins in the light of their modern truth and, in so doing, absolve themselves. They say, "Jesus loves me; that is truth. It doesn't matter what I do. As long Jesus loves me, it frees me of guilt."

This second statement misses the whole point.

The truth of which John speaks when quoting Jesus is the same today as it was two thousand years ago. The never-mentioned prior verse—Verse 31—says it simply, "If you follow my teachings." Simply put, the truths referred to are the teachings of Christ. This truth—the teachings of Christ—is that which sets us free. Christ and God do indeed love all of us, but our obedience is also crucial to our salvation. Those who believe they can live a life of sin and rely solely on God's love will find themselves surprised on the day of their own judgment.

Christ tells his disciples that we are all slaves of sin, and slaves are not members of the family but something less. However, if we follow his teaching and accept him as our Lord and Savior who died for our sins, we will be freed by the Son of God from the bondage of sin. Then, we will become members of the holy family.

But to be free, you must not only know the Jesus teachings; you must follow the Jesus teachings.

Yes, Christ broke bread with sinners, but he did so precisely because they were sinners. He searched them out. Sitting with them, he neither ignored their sin nor condoned it, but endeavored to save them from their path to more sin. Like a good shepherd, these people were the lost sheep he wished to save. Remember in John 8:1-11: When the woman was about to be stoned, and he rebuked the crowd, challenging that he who was without sin to cast that first stone, he was not condoning her past sin but forgiving her for them. Key to this biblical story is her repentance for her sin. His following words are the key: "Go, and sin no more" (v. 11 KJV).

That is the part so many people forget today. It is not enough to know we are sinners. That knowledge is where the truth starts, but not where it ends. We must confront our sin, acknowledge it, accept Jesus into our hearts, and then, in seeking forgiveness, "Go, and sin no more."

People today might face their sins and perhaps even explicitly acknowledge them, but almost everyone forgets the last half of the sentence. Yet it is that last bit that sets us free, and it is precisely this we must never forget.

CHAPTER 7

Another Conversation

"After three days they [Mary and Joseph] found him [Jesus] in the temple courts, sitting among the teachers, listening to them and asking them questions."—Luke 2:46 NIV

An author friend of mine will not like this book. You might ask how I know. Simple. He read a manuscript of mine years ago and hated the ending. I finished that book not by wrapping everything up nicely but with a question to the reader.

"It's not a French novel," he scolded me at the time. "A story has a beginning, a middle, and an end. Imagine you've brought the reader on a flight, gotten the plane to the edge of the runway, and then dropped them there. No, you've got to land the plane. You must finish the story."

I got the point, although secretly, I disagreed with him. However, he was a published author, and I was not. What he said made sense, at least from a commercial perspective, and the advice came from a place of experience, but nothing is ever so simple or artificial for me. The truth is, no story truly ever ends. What finishes one chapter in a person's life inevitably leads to the next.

Who among us ever has such a conveniently tidy tale? Who among us has a single story with a beginning, a middle, and an end? We all have a beginning and, ultimately, an end. In between, we have many tales; they overlap, and many remain without a conclusion, even at our own endings. They are seldom neat or well-ordered, and rarely are they tidy.

Everyone's stories continue, with our moments overlapping, woven together in a complex tapestry. The end of one story of mine might be the beginning for someone else. But that is only on this earth, in this life, and before we pass on to our judgment before God.

For years, I confess I did not give that concept much thought. I had long ago decided I was unworthy of salvation. After all, I'd had a front-row seat to the production that was my life. I knew all that I had done. I was intimately aware of my sins, the wrongs I'd committed, and the lack of compassion I'd had unabashedly on full display. I had looked at my ledger many times, and in accounting terms, I had achieved total depreciation. In short, I had written myself off.

It was not that I did not believe in Christ. No, I have been a believer—or thought of myself as such—for more than half a century. But as you will read later, I had, until recently, been a casual Christian, and if I haven't already made myself clear, not a very good one.

Then God spoke to me.

He said, "I am the house in which you can find shelter. If you walk a different path, you will find yourself subject to the winds, rains, and storms. Come to me and find protection from the world around you. I am the shelter in which you will find protection from the storm. Follow me and walk upon my path, and you will find the way clear, but if you wander off out of my sight, you will become lost and unable to find your way. Trust in me, for I am the Lord."

In response to this, I posed a series of questions. These were not to challenge God but to learn. My instruction was beginning.

Me: How do I know you are God and not Satan?

God: Because I come in peace, to bring you peace. I tell you to do no harm, to be better. Satan would not deceive you so. Satan would offer the riches of this world just as he did Jesus. I offer you the wealth of eternal life. He would not encourage you to do what is right. Instead, he would tell you that wrong is right. He would not say do not sin. He would say there is no such thing as sin. I understand your concern. Satan cannot offer you a path to salvation, for salvation can only be found in my truth. As my son said, "Can Satan cast out Satan?"

You think, "Am I just talking to myself?" To this, I say no. If this were so, you would be giving yourself comforting answers that would not hold you to account. You would hear answers that would appeal to your mortal and human nature. You would listen to voices making pitiful excuses for your sins and not providing answers aimed at saving your eternal soul. Have I not proven myself to you? Have you not been seen? Believe and have faith.

Me: I worry about my past.

God: You have sought forgiveness, and Jesus has given it to you. Can you not see the changes within you? You had no compassion or empathy, but now you are different. You have a great distance yet to travel, it is true. But do not think I do not see you have changed, and I am pleased.

Me: But I cannot help but think about sinning.

God: I understand. I started to explain this earlier. You cannot control your thoughts. They come in the blink of an eye. They are upon you before you know it. They even come to you in your sleep. What is important in the first instance is that you can control your reaction to those thoughts, and you can control what you do with those thoughts. You do not have to act on them, and you must not.

You may have done so in the past, but now, in asking for my forgiveness through Jesus, you have been forgiven. As for today, if you experience sinful thoughts, renounce them and ask forgiveness. You strive to be better than you have been. You are growing. You are human, and this is the best you can do.

Christ said, "Ye have heard that it was said by them of old time, Thou shalt not commit adultery: But I say unto you, That whosoever looketh on a woman to lust after her hath committed adultery with her already in his heart" (Matthew 5:27-28 KJV).

It is important to remember why he said that. Man cannot help that he sins; it is your nature. What is more important is what comes after sin. You ask for forgiveness and try not to sin again. You will, but you can try not to, and each time, you must pray about it, contemplate it, ask forgiveness, and move forward. What is important in these situations is remembering not to act on your sinful thoughts.

You have also been thinking, "Why is sin, as opposed to what is sin?" To that, I say, sin—especially those sins only pondered—is the trapdoor through which Satan enters your soul. It is one matter to address a direct challenge to your faith. Still, these trapdoors, once opened through the commission of internal or covert sin—including simple thought—allow Satan to gain a foothold that can misdirect your faith, turn you from the truth, and tempt you with the secular world over my heavenly kingdom.

This is why thought sins are so dangerous, because the idle thought is something you may dismiss out of hand and not even realize you have left a way open to betray your own soul. This is the evil, insidious nature of Satan, who works his will through the thoughts of man. This is why it is crucial to understand that, ultimately, all sins begin in men's minds. For every overt act, there precedes an idea, for good or ill. This is where Satan and I wage our eternal struggle.

Satan will always try every moment of every day of your life. His methods are subtle and devious, and he never stops; never. This is why your vigilance must always be high. If there is any good in all that, imagine how important you must be to him that he seeks you so.

Me: Nothing is forever, not even miracles.

God: Nothing of your existence in this world you occupy is forever. Any miracle, even one that lasts for a lifetime, necessarily ends with your life. Nothing is eternal except eternity, and for now, that exists only in heaven. It is true that one day, the two—heaven and earth—will become one, but that time has not yet come; it is not yet time. You will not see that day until the two are reborn.

The miraculous acts I perform for you and through you are my gift to you and are not something you earn. It is a privilege and not an automatic reward of any kind. They are gifts predicated only on whether I choose to work through you.

Again, you must understand that two people may perform the same deed, and one will be deemed pleasing and the other less so. This is because the act is greater than the mere deed. In simplest terms, if one does something worthwhile and does it with a pure heart, they will find favor in my eyes. Yet another may do the same thing and do so only with the expectation of a reward or worldly acknowledgement. If the reward is expected in this world, then they have sacrificed their reward in heaven.

It was so with Cain and Abel, and it is still so today. Remember, I know your every thought. I know your heart and your true intentions, always.

CHAPTER 8

A Conversation on Purpose

"But I have raised you up for this very purpose, that I might show you my power and that my name might be proclaimed in all the earth."
—Exodus 9:16 NIV

A continuing theme in my talks with God revolves around depression. I don't know if I meet the definition of clinically depressed, for I've never asked. Life always seemed full of challenges, accomplishments, and destinations reached. I never afforded myself the luxury of enjoying the journey. It was always about the destination.

In that regard, I considered myself normal. Many people, most I would say, are more concerned about reaching the finish line. That's the point: to get where you're going quickly and with as few errors as possible. I always envied those who could stop and enjoy the moment, but I was never sure what that meant.

I have tried. I've stood at the edge of the Grand Canyon and tried to take in its majesty. I've looked out over the skyline of Manhattan from the Empire State Building, hoping to absorb the spectacle. I've done the same thing countless times in countless locations, but none stirred my soul. I had reached the mountaintop, but when I'd arrived, all I could ask myself was, "How do I get down?"

As I end my sixth decade, I did not care much about anything anymore. Those things that once might have moved me no longer did so. Food had lost its flavor, and sleep had become merely periods of profound unconsciousness from which I awoke neither refreshed nor revived. The interest was no longer there, whether it was a friendship or a football game. I lost touch with what friends I did have because I had run out of things to say. There wasn't anything new to add to my life's adventure. There were no more battles worth winning, no more dragons to slay. As I watched my father grow old, I saw these same things happen to him. Then, I did not understand. Now I do.

With the road toward the end of his life shortening, he looked backward, not forward. I understood, and it made logical sense. When you move nearer to your destination—especially the ultimate, final destination—you have nothing to do but look back on the journey. However, as I watched him, I came to this same realization about myself. I discovered that I didn't recall much of the journey. What would I have to look back on?

It was as if I had been on an express train, and the landscape had been flying past me at breakneck speed. I found I could not remember some past event in my life more than I could remember some pasture I'd see outside the train window. It was all an abstract. It was all, in fact, devoid of any emotion.

From this frame of reference, I approached a brief conversation with God.

"God," I whispered as I lay in bed. It was dark, just before sunrise. "God, what is the matter with me?"

"Tell me what you mean," I heard God reply.

I had long ago discovered the Lord prefers the Socratic method. He knew perfectly well what I meant. His question prompted me to search for the answer from within.

"I don't feel anything anymore. Nothing matters anymore."

"And why do you think that is?"

"I don't know," I sighed. "It just seems like that. I mean, what's the point? Nothing on this earth matters. Heaven is eternal. That's what

Christians dream about. That's what matters. We all want to go to heaven. Everything else is prologue."

"Do you believe in me?"

"Yes, you know I do."

"Tell me, how can you believe in me yet not in what I do?"

"What do you mean?"

"Did I not create everything around you? Did I not create the earth beneath your feet? Did I not create you?"

"Yes, of course you did."

"And do you think I have nothing better to do? Do you think what I do is unimportant?"

"No," I stammered. "Of course not."

"Well, then, if you believe in me and in my plan, and if you think that what I do is important, then why do you not value what I am doing and the gifts I have given to you and all humanity?"

For that, I had no answer. I just sat quietly and thought about what he had said. "What is the point, then? What am I missing?"

"You are missing a purpose—a reason for being. You are wasting your life on things that do not matter. You fight daily battles, most of which you cannot win. And when you do win, these victories mean nothing, for they are for naught. What matters most is spreading the word and truth of who and what I am, and what all mankind can be, if it chooses to be so."

"Of course, that is all well and good, but what purpose—what role—could I have in that? What could I do that would matter?"

"You are doing it now, and you don't even see it."

"What?"

"You are talking to me. This is a gift, a blessing if you will. Use it, shape it, put it to good use. I have shown you miracles. I have given you many gifts. Our conversations, for one. Your writing skills for another. Put them together. You have played with your writing, on and off, to some good use, but now I charge you with doing something more. Use these gifts to honor my name."

CHAPTER 9

God and the Lottery

"Be strong and courageous. Do not be afraid or terrified because of them, for the Lord your God goes with you; he will never leave you nor forsake you."—Deuteronomy 31:6 NIV

About a year ago, I began talking to God about my finances. I once underwent a sudden financial reversal. While that was years ago, now I find as I grow older that I constantly worry about surviving in today's world. Would I earn enough to see me through to the end of my life? I worried that if I needed to return to work, I would be virtually unemployable despite a lifetime of success. In my mid-sixties in today's world, I saw no way to function without being able to earn a living.

I also found myself wondering if God grew weary of my whining about the subject. He had repeatedly told me I must not worry about such things, and he had long ago said as much in Joshua 1:9: "Have not I commanded thee? Be strong and of a good courage; be not afraid, neither be thou dismayed: for the Lord thy God is with thee whithersoever thou goest" (KJV).

I only offer that verse because I keep it on my desktop computer. As I have said, I have not committed the Bible to memory. I do not have that gift, but I digress.

"I promise you this," he whispered in response to my pleas. "You do not need to worry about money. But I do not promise you that you will have no worries. There will be challenges but concerns about that will not be among them."

At first, I took that at face value and found great comfort in what he had said. And true to his word, money flowed into my life. It did not come in vast amounts, but it was sufficient to meet my needs, and I understood that, as it says repeatedly in Proverbs, I must be prudent and wise with what was made available to me.

Only months later did it occur to me the possible implications of what God had said and what he might have meant. Perhaps I needn't worry because I would be dying soon. If so, what of my wife? I have life insurance, so she would be fine for a time, but I thought of her family and their exceptionally long lifespans. She could live another thirty years. I knew that what I would leave her wouldn't be enough. The worrying began again, and I complained to God again, wishing I could win the lottery. I told myself that would take care of all my concerns and that I would have plenty to give to the church. Surely, that would please him.

Once again, I heard from the Lord.

"So," he said evenly. "It would please you to win the lottery?"

"Yes," I replied hopefully as I began counting the winnings I felt sure would follow.

"Very well. Tell me, would you be willing to trade five years of your life for it?"

"I don't understand," I said cautiously.

"I mean, would you be willing to die five years earlier than you should otherwise in exchange for winning?"

I considered his suggestion for a moment. My parents had lived long lives; my father was ninety-one, and my mother was ninety. That would still give me at least another twenty-five years, and in all honesty, their last few years were not pleasant anyway. I calculated I could "live" without those last years.

"Sure," I finally volunteered.

Then God said, "Now let me ask you another question. How do you know how long you are to live? How do you know you aren't supposed to die five years and one day from today? I know the answer, but you don't. Are you willing to take that risk?"

Immediately, I saw his point. How could I know? I had just assumed I would live as long as my parents. What if I were wrong?

"On second thought," I answered sheepishly, "I wouldn't make that trade."

"Very well then. Now, I want you to think about something else."

"What?"

"What do you think about when you think about winning the lottery? Do you think about how you'd spend it? What you would buy yourself? Or how good you would feel not having to worry about surviving day-to-day?"

"Yes," I admitted finally, "but I guess you already know that much, don't you?"

"Of course. I am God, after all. Now, let me ask you another question. Do you find comfort in such thoughts?"

"Yes."

"Even though the odds of winning are three hundred million-to-one?"

"Yes."

"And yet you sometimes find it easier to believe in the lottery than in me. I want you to think about that."

That thought stunned me. I found comfort in daydreaming about winning a three hundred million-to-one chance, yet I could not find continued comfort in the Lord's word even when it was plainly revealed to me. This realization had indeed opened my eyes. So many times, people express a belief in intangible things, yet they also, like I once did, have lingering doubts about God. Some believe in Satan or in demons, and yet they find a belief in God ridiculous. Others believe in UFOs or ancient aliens with no proof and yet laugh at Christians for being naive.

The miracles in my life reminded me of God's existence. I feel that

I have infinitely more "proof" of God than nonbelievers do in games of chance. They just need to open their eyes and their hearts to the possibility of what a difference God can make in their lives.

It becomes a matter of where one puts one's faith.

Chapter 10

A Glass of Water

"And the dust returns to the ground it came from, and the spirit returns to God who gave it."—Ecclesiastes 12:7 NIV

The Sermon on the Mount is one of the many biblical stories I grew up reading. As children in Sunday school, it became central to our faith. Within those verses is the heart and soul of Christianity, and Jesus's teachings place the path to heaven plainly before us.

Implicit in his words is the understanding that man exists on a physical and a spiritual plane, two in one. While I grasped his words on an emotional level, I could not help but question them logically. This world was my existence, and until recently, I could not imagine any other, regardless of what the scriptures say.

Recently, though, as I prayed to God about finding my way through the day-to-day burdens of this life, I thought again about Jesus's words. I asked him for understanding—how could we not be concerned about our reality as living beings?

As I muttered sarcastically, "The lilies of the field don't pay rent."

I am no longer shocked when he answers me, but when he does, I confess I sometimes do not comprehend his meaning.

"You are all so much more than a creature of the world you occupy," God said to me. "You possess a soul that transcends this existence. Honestly, it is more important than your physical self."

"How could a person's soul exist separate from their body?" I wondered. "Were we not one thing?"

"Take a glass," he responded simply, knowing my thoughts, "and fill it with water."

I did so, and he told me to examine it.

"What do you see?"

"A glass of water," I replied, stating the obvious.

He then instructed me to pour the water out. Again, I did so.

Then he repeated the question to me. "What do you see?"

"An empty glass," I replied.

"And did the water cease to exist?"

"No," I said, looking at the puddle at my feet.

"The glass is the vessel—the body—and the water is the soul—the essence of who and what you are. Why is it so easy to understand a glass of water but not comprehend your own existence? The water can remain in the glass, or it can be poured out. Its existence does not depend upon the glass. The water is each person's soul; the glass, like your body, is merely a vessel. It breaks and is discarded, but the water has many forms, and it never ceases to exist."

It was a revelation. I had never viewed life and existence that way before, and in that instant, I felt I grasped at least a little of our true selves.

He repeated to me then, as he had said before, "Did I not create you in my image? Do you think your physical body is the entire sum and substance of what you are?"

"No," I replied, "but this existence is all I can see."

As I thought about what he had revealed to me, I remembered reading a biography of Albert Einstein and his discussions on the limitations of observing matter. I wonder if Einstein did not somehow grasp the same thing I was coming to see. He did not discuss it as a matter of religion but one of scientific observation.

These thoughts brought me to the subsequent realization. I asked

God if this is the nature of man. If, as he said, we are both the glass and the water, does that mean we cannot see the true nature of the universe in our current physical state?

"After all," I said, thinking of the puddle before me, "when the water is in the glass, it cannot observe the ground, and when it is on the ground it cannot see the glass."

Were we, by virtue of being based within these three dimensions, limited to seeing these dimensions?

God chuckled slightly. "You are correct," he said finally, "or at least as correct as could be comprehended by you in this life. Of course, you are not able to change your observations. You are fixed within this existence. That only changes when you leave this life behind. Now our next conversation is, why? Why are you here? What is to be gained by your narrow ability to observe, as you put it, the limits of your existence?"

I shrugged my shoulders. On that subject, I had absolutely no idea.

"Do not feel confused. I do not expect you to know or understand. You are not meant to see beyond this horizon. You cannot, and I do not expect you to try. It is enough to believe, and I will show you the way in time. That is the meaning of faith. Faith is trust. Trust in me. Trust in what I tell you and what I inspire you to write down. You might be amazed to find that the words you write down will one day move the world."

It was then I recalled this verse from Isaiah 12:2: "Surely God is my salvation; I will trust and not be afraid. The Lord, the Lord himself, is my strength and my defense; he has become my salvation" (NIV).

CHAPTER 11

Thoughts on Consciousness

"Let us make mankind in our image, in our likeness."
—Genesis 1:26 NIV

In considering my lesson on the duality of man, I thought of Albert Einstein's thesis on the limitations of humanity's ability to observe this world. God had said I was correct, at least as far as I could be correct in this life. This thought, I felt, required further exploration. What follows is a more scientific approach to the question: a hypothesis, if you will. God does not bless my approach, yet neither is its discussion forbidden.

What if our consciousness exists on a multidimensional, quantum level while our physical beings remain rooted within this singular three-dimensional existence? What if the brain functions on a quantum level? What if this fact gives rise to our consciousness? What if, because of the quantum nature of our existence, we cannot observe the objective truth of that existence?

Granted, these are all "what ifs," but consider the possibilities and implications of these simple-sounding questions for a moment. The answers could give a rational basis to faith and explain much about God, human existence, and experience. Surprisingly, there is scientific evidence that might back up this hypothesis.

Briefly, quantum theory is a study of physics at the subatomic level. It differs radically from traditional physics, which is the basis of our shared reality. Among other things, quantum theory allows discrete particles to exist in different realities simultaneously.

Consider this fascinating example from the field of quantum physics. Protons in light exist in two simultaneous but different realities, both as discrete particles and as waves. These are the dual properties of photons. However, one cannot observe both realities simultaneously. Why? Because the act of choosing what to observe dictates—and thus limits—your observation.

This example suggests to me that we cannot observe the entire reality of our existence because the mere fact of observing our existence interferes with any complete observation of that existence. In the scientific world, this concept is known as the Heisenberg Uncertainty Principle, which posits that it is impossible to precisely measure a particle's position and momentum simultaneously. The "Schrodinger's Cat" thought experiment illustrates the most famous example of this concept of quantum superposition, which states that if you put a cat in a box with poison gas, it is simultaneously both alive and dead until you open the box and make an observation. In more mundane language, it suggests a particle exists in multiple states until observed.

In other words, we cannot observe an experiment in which we play a part because our very presence affects the reality we choose. To understand our reality completely, we must be outside that reality. God can observe us because he is outside our plane of existence. He can, therefore, choose to involve himself in our lives and affect the nature of our collective realities. He can, in essence, change the nature or parameters of the experiment.

I do not know if this speculation on quantum physics is correct—no one can. But I do find it an exciting possibility.

CHAPTER 12

The Devil Comes at 3:00 a.m.

"The coming of the lawless one will be in accordance with how Satan works. He will use all sorts of displays of power through signs and wonders that serve the lie."—2 Thessalonians 2:9 NIV

The devil comes at 3:00 a.m. It is true. He wraps himself within the dark tapestry of the night's stillness and softly encourages the doubts reverberating within my mind. He lingers in the shadows, reminding me of all my sins, now long past and yet still so well remembered. All the lies I've told, the things I either did or did not do, and the pains I've caused, both great and small. All these things creep into my suddenly alert consciousness.

The devil knows what I am thinking, and I know he knows. My mind cannot resist the bitter regrets he dangles before me, and once more, we stumble together down the twisted, winding pathway of my past. The trail is briar-filled, uneven, and unsure. With each mental misstep, I recall another forgotten wrong I have committed.

I count the years and the sins and pray time lessens the guilt, although I know it does not. The pain is strange, bitterly exquisite, and he knows that once again, I cannot help but listen to his words. It is a song sung slightly off-key, yet alluring nonetheless. I find myself cringing, wanting to turn away but unable to do so.

Then, suddenly, he tempts me with my secret desires. He tempts me with them like sweet pastries he knows I will devour. He offers me these morsels so I may freely choose whichever sinful delights I wish. He alternates between the weakness of my past sin and the promise of sins yet to come, trying to pry me from my Lord.

Each night, the flashbacks begin at the beginning, in my teens, and I witness within my mind every sin, transgression, lie, and misstep of my life. He forces me to see these moments without censor. The purpose is clear.

The devil challenges me. "Your God lets you punish yourself, to remember your—what does he call them—transgressions. Why? So you beg him for forgiveness and protection. Do you know what God is really saying? He is saying, 'You are mine, and your whole life is mine. You must pay homage to me. To be forgiven, you must worship me.' Ask yourself, why would an all-powerful being need your exaltation? Why does he demand you bow down to him?"

I listen to his words. I try not to, but I see the parade within my mind, and I cannot disagree with him. I see what the devil sees; I wince as he laughs, enjoying my suffering. I listen to Satan's words of supposed comfort, and they sound vaguely like those of a snake oil salesman. They are full of high hopes and unkept promises.

Yet the weight of these many years continues to press down upon me. It was—it is—a painful display. I wince involuntarily with each thought, and I see what he means. I am unworthy, and I know it. We both do.

Then he attempts to comfort me. "I do not laugh at you. I laugh at the folly of believing God grants you some fake pardon for simply living your life for him. I do not demand your goodness," he hisses. "No. It is the opposite. Your God revels in judging your sin. I tell you, what you feel is not the pain of sin but the pain of failure, of trying to live to impossible demands."

Then, he tries a different track. He challenges me to explain what sin is. Why is my life an example of corruption?

"You are not perfect. That much we both know," he whispers. "But that's all right. You were never intended to be so. I will not judge you. Your God intended you humans to be nothing more than slaves, captive worshippers, whose silly reward for serving on bended knee is to spend eternity bowing and scraping before a God craving adoration."

He lets these thoughts sink in and continues, "You have it in you to be so much more. Your kind has no idea what you are truly capable of. God does, and you know what? It scares him. If you renounce God and follow me, I will show you a better way. One that allows you to build on your true strengths and not have to forever seek forgiveness."

I paused at that sudden alien thought. I asked myself, who had I been praying to all this time? Who had been answering my prayers? Who had been comforting me? All this time, have I been talking to God, or Satan, or even, perhaps, just to myself?

It was then I heard another voice, one familiar and comforting.

"Begone, Satan," I heard God say. "This one walks within the protection of my light, safe from your evil ways."

"You needn't tell me," replied the devil. "But you might want to remind your mortal creature. If he truly believed he was yours, then our conversation would not be necessary."

"You can say that? You, who tried to tempt even my Son. Begone."

It felt strange hearing myself talked about in the third person, especially as I was the only person in the room. Was I going mad? At that moment, I did not know.

Now—today—I know I'm not, and honestly, even then, I did not think so.

We have all heard it said that if one can question their sanity, they probably aren't insane, but honestly, lying in bed at 3:00 a.m., it is hard to be absolutely sure.

Then, God reassured me.

"Do not worry," he whispered gently. "You are sane, and you are not alone. I am with you always. I know all that is happening is difficult for you to grasp and perhaps sometimes even to believe. Satan and I are locked in an eternal struggle for the soul of man. He is jealous of you. He envies my love for you, and he cannot comprehend it, no matter how hard he tries. To keep us apart, he will offer you anything, but he only promises lies. His way leads to eternal chaos and damnation. I offer you eternal peace. Trust in me and have faith."

    And I do.

CHAPTER 13

Knowledge and Wisdom

"Give me wisdom and knowledge, that I may lead this people, for who is able to govern this great people of yours?"—2 Chronicles 1:10 NIV

As I have said before, I am not a Bible verse guy. I learned basic Christian concepts in my youth, not chapters and verses. That doesn't matter nowadays, not with Google readily available. If you know a few of the words, you can find anything.

In this case, though, I recalled one of my favorite verses, Proverbs 3:5-6: "Trust in the Lord with all your heart and lean not on your own understanding; in all your ways submit to him, and he will make your paths straight" (NIV).

This passage speaks to me about several things, the first and most obvious being the nature of faith because trust requires faith. It embodies the most basic meaning of our shared belief in God: Trust in the Lord. That thought is repeated so many times in the Bible because, throughout history, we have had a track record of second-guessing God. We know what we want or think we want, and if we are honest with ourselves, we know what God wants and thinks, especially when it's different from our own.

This same verse reminds us not to trust our knowledge and understanding. This implies something equally obvious: Our human understanding is both fallible and limited. More importantly, by extension, it tells us we must have the humility and self-awareness to realize that fact. We should humble ourselves before God and accept there is something greater, something more all-encompassing than ourselves. This brings us to the final point; it requires us to acknowledge that we cannot know God's plan, either in scope or depth, nor can we anticipate it.

In short, we must have faith.

In this regard, one of many questions I have pondered is the fall from grace in the Garden of Eden and the Tree of Knowledge. Satan tempted Eve, and she, in turn, tempted Adam. That much we all know, whether or not one believes in an actual or metaphorical Eden. Whether the story is a fact or a parable, it is self-contained. Man was a simple creature, and the point remains the same whether he wandered in a garden called Eden or whether Eden was the entire world.

Humanity is God's creation. We exist within the world and as a part of the world. It was when man gained knowledge that his relationship with the world changed. This newly acquired knowledge separated him from his Lord and his world.

Consider for a moment the scientist's view of Earth and creation. I can accept the concept of evolution, but it is objectively obvious that something transformative happened to the species scientifically known as Homo sapiens sapiens. We have discovered more, become more, and advanced more in the past ten thousand years than in the previous three hundred thousand. That speaks to our gaining knowledge of ourselves and the world around us.

We have also become more dangerous, wasteful, murderous, and self-serving creatures. That speaks to the fact that while we gained knowledge, there was no corresponding gaining of wisdom. It appears that knowledge, like eating the apple, came in a galactic instant. Just as clearly, wisdom did not.

I would suggest the two are not connected for a simple reason. While knowledge can be given, wisdom must be earned. If it is not earned, it has no value to those who acquire it. They do not appreciate it any more than an infant who inherits a billion dollars will understand the value of his newfound wealth and its meaning to those less fortunate.

Our sudden advancement in knowledge, which should have moved us to new heights, is destroying us. But can this logical progression hint at anything concerning God's plan for us?

I would say yes.

I think our purpose on this earth is to learn and grow. God wishes us to learn the value of faith and a belief in that which we can never see in this life. Whatever God's greater plan, it seems that part of his purpose is for us to learn from our failures and gain wisdom because this is the only way we can grow.

We may feel the warmth of a fire and see its light as it flickers on the walls, but we can only learn that fire will burn us if we try to touch its flames. Putting our hand in the flames the first time is knowledge; not doing it again is wisdom.

Chapter 14

Cause and Effect

"Truly he is my rock and my salvation; he is my fortress; I will never be shaken."—Psalm 62:2 NIV

Do you become closer to God and abandon sin, or do you abandon sin to come closer to God? Which comes first, the chicken or the egg? For me, it was the former. I found that as I grew closer to God, I felt less drawn to the ways of my sinful past.

There was a time when I cringed at the memory of my past. Even now, I take no pride in things I've done, but I find such thoughts more tolerable with my growing relationship with God. It is not to say I have forgotten my sins. Far from it—I will never forget them. Perhaps I am not supposed to, even if God has. It is like the old saying, "Those who forget the lessons of the past are doomed to repeat them."

I do know, however, that God has forgiven me of my past. He did that by putting his Son on the cross. In doing so, Jesus died so I might have God's grace and eternal life.

What is more important, the past or the future? While I once willingly committed myself to things in the past, those desires no longer tempt or haunt me.

Once, I freely chose to do the things I did, but now I have no desire to continue down that road. The less-traveled path that leads me to God also leads me away from sin. I found God while in the full flower of my darkness. I came to him broken and battered, burdened by the things I'd done. I could not forgive myself, and I could not forget. Half-joking, I used to tell people I would not embarrass God by asking for forgiveness. I was a lost cause, and I would not deny it. That was my hell, and I was going there at breakneck speed. I had made that bed, and accepting the fate I had created for myself seemed the most honorable course.

Then, with acceptance of God and Jesus, the light rose in my darkness, and night gave way to dawn. I did not come to him purified but putrid. Not clean but layered in filth. I understand now why Jesus sat with the sinners and tax collectors. Because nowhere was he more desperately needed than among those whom Jesus wished to save. He was not there because he approved of the wrongs they had committed but to save them from themselves. His purpose was not to rebuke but to offer the opportunity for salvation.

Thus it was with me, also. I did not begin to work on my sins in the hope of gaining salvation. Instead, I gained salvation, and at that moment, my sinful desires lessened. They did not completely vanish, but I no longer wished to act without considering my actions. It was like an alcoholic who suddenly lost the desire to drink. And like that recovering alcoholic, while I had no more desire to sin, I would always be a sinner. Still, I no longer carried those burdens from my past.

Being released from my sins and guilt, I also discovered a new humility. In my youth, I had been arrogant and self-centered. Now, I longed to be less judgmental. How could I accept being forgiven of my sins and not be willing to forgive others?

Of course, there are things that, as Christians, we must be mindful of within ourselves and others. I cannot absolve others of their sins; that is not my job. However, I can help those who wish for absolution find their way. This relates to the verse I mentioned before to help people find the truth, to go forth and sin no more.

Jesus also called on men to judge not, lest we be judged ourselves by the scales of our judgment of others (Matthew 7:1-3). This, though, is not the judgmental behavior I refer to in people. We judge people for actions violating our standards, not God's. We judge their hairstyles, their weight, their appearance. In short, we judge all the things that we do not like or approve of in others.

How can we expect to receive a pardon from our particular judgment and not strive to do the same to our fellow man?

Chapter 15

Faith

"Have faith in God."—Mark 11:22 NIV

Here is an awkward little truth: We all need faith. I do not mean we should like to have it or be willing to discuss it. I mean, we all need it.

Faith—believing in something greater than ourselves that we cannot prove and yet accept as truth—is something for which we all long. Our souls require faith as much as our bodies require food, water, and air. For me, that something is God. It should be what you believe in as well.

There are those who deny this basic fact—atheists. They protest there is no such imperative. Have you heard the old saying that there are no atheists in foxholes? What today's atheists cannot bring themselves to acknowledge is that life itself is one giant foxhole.

Those who live without believing in something greater than themselves will one day face a tragic reality. We all must find something more meaningful than ourselves. The simple fact is that faith gives us purpose and meaning; without it, our very existence becomes pointless, aimless, and chaotic. The most basic truth is that if God did not exist, we would have created him. Fortunately, he does exist. Mankind desperately needs to look to him if our lives are to have any real meaning.

It is a fundamental axiom—first voiced by the English poet Robert Browning—that our reach should exceed our grasp, but why? We remember the first part of that quote, but do you know the rest? It goes, "Or what's a heaven for?" Browning grasped that in mankind's striving to be the best we all can be, we must strive for more than we already are.

Another word for faith could be religion, but the two are not synonymous. God is perfect. Man is not. Do not fall into the trap of believing that if a pastor fails, a priest fails, or even a church fails, then believing in God must also fail. One is not the other. The concept of an immortal God survives our mortal attempts because while he is perfect, we are not.

Still, if you are not yet ready to address belief in God emotionally, then consider that there is a philosophical reason to believe. Religion, however imperfect, provides the structure by which we live. Mankind needs these conceptualizations—call them absolutes, if you wish—that delineate a commonly shared outline and borders of what we mean by normal, civilized behavior.

Without such guideposts, we become undisciplined, complacent, and morally corpulent. Our virtues become defined in secular, relativistic terms. As Christ put it, our houses would be built on sand. What is moral and right for you may be immoral for me or vice versa. Marriage: Is it just between a single man and a single woman, or between men and women, men and men, or women and women? Are unborn lives sacred and given by God, or not? Why would any one person's life be significant, and who would decide?

The choices go on from there. Over time, a changing culture slowly moves away from faith to chaos, from one generation to the next, until one day, that core set of faith-based values that once made us a civilization vanish in a misbegotten humanistic dream, and everyone is at peril.

Unlike religion, while it indeed suffers from human frailty in delivering its epistle, secular philosophies are erroneous from their very inception. They offer a shallow, self-serving message in search of a weak and willing messenger. The simple fact is that the relativistic, humanistic approach always fails. It fails because, while faith encourages humanity to the heights of shared sacrifice for the common good, undisciplined secular motives drive us inexorably face-to-face with humanity's lowest common denominator. It fails because humans are fallible, and we will ultimately fall far short when we look solely within ourselves. Where religion challenges us to be something more, humanism says it is okay to accept who we are, just as we are. Instead of being overcome, our sins are to be accepted or even celebrated. In short, when we replace God's will with our own, we move from humility to hubris.

Another human shortcoming is our shared predilection for simultaneously seeing the best in ourselves and the worst in others. This shortcoming is precisely what Christ addressed when he spoke at the Sermon on the Mount. When we make rules from a purely humanistic approach, we intend their imposition on others, not for ourselves—never for ourselves. This fact plays out today in the oft-chanted line, "Rules for thee, but not for me."

This ability for self-delusion shows its face when the elites in any society invariably decide that they, as society's most educated and enlightened humans, know better than everyone else. They believe they are uniquely suited and situated to pass judgment on the actions of others, the great "unwashed" of humanity.

They fail to understand that there is nothing to support them in their search for some higher moral purpose except their own finite perceptions. Such a society may profess the highest ideals, but the absence of faith leaves them without the structure to either achieve or sustain true ideals. In contrast, while religion may seem to also suffer from the same failing, at least the fact of God's perfection points at those failing as they happen. Humanism does not.

For a society to grow and thrive, it must have absolutes that support and guide it. Whether it's something as controversial as abortion or as mundane as the United States Constitution, our benchmarks must be immoveable, not subject to the slippery slope of the lazy, distracted, or unmotivated individuals who eventually somehow come together en masse to choose the seemingly most straightforward option, precisely because it is just that.

Why does this happen? Because faith carries with it many other things that inevitably flow from it. Faith, and therefore, religion, brings with it a set of moral standards. These standards require self-discipline. Faith, in turn, both requires and promotes character, allowing people to weather hardships, whether building a single life or a civilization. This is the causal chain that builds inexorably on faith.

Without religious faith to provide a bedrock foundation, morality suffers, self-discipline falters, and character becomes relative. Then, abortion becomes merely a matter of personal choice, and our inalienable, God-given rights become subject to the bureaucratic whim of the state.

When we follow that path, the granite bedrock of our faith gives way to the sandstone of humanism, and society falls back to the earth like a progressively leaning tower.

Chapter 16

Having Faith in Your Purpose

"Even after Jesus had performed so many signs in their presence, they still would not believe in him."
—John 12:37 NIV

My pastor seemingly has an unerring ability to talk directly to me. I know that's not true, but it sure feels that way. While intellectually, I know he is preaching to all in the congregation, I sometimes cannot help but believe that God directs his message in my direction.

On one such occasion, he spoke of adversity and having the strength to have faith in God's purpose for us, even when we feel uncertain. Earlier that same morning, as I stood alone in my home, I thought about how tired I was of everything around me—tired of the worry, tired of the stress, and just plain tired of living. I wasn't suicidal, but I did feel like I was at the point of giving up. As Pastor Jon said later, I was struggling with the darkness.

As luck would have it, this was the sense of despair that was the object of his sermon that day. He reminded me that God has a purpose for everything that happens. Whenever something happens to us, even if it is simply fatigue, we must remember that out of this darkness comes the dawn of a new day filled with God's promise.

I must continually remind myself that my timeline is not God's. An infinite and eternal being will not have the same frame of reference as a mortal man. If we're lucky, we live sixty, seventy, and even eighty years or more. If we're lucky, still, that is less than the blink of an eye for God. What is a lifetime to us is less than a moment to him. Couple that fact with the infinite span of his vision, and it is difficult, if not at times impossible, for us to comprehend the scope of his vision.

I have come to see that regardless of our momentary difficulties, whenever placed in moments of adversity, we all ultimately have a part in God's greater plan, and we are always placed here for some purpose greater than ourselves.

Think of Damar Hamlin, the football player who suffered a heart attack during a nationally televised game in 2023. At that moment, a coincidental combination of factors—a perfectly timed collision, an impact at just the right spot, his heart beating at just the right pace—and in an instant, a man most of America did not know lay dying on the field before a national television audience.

Suddenly, a nation remembered how to pray. Both teams came together and knelt on the field in prayer, and the cameras neither turned away nor turned off. They did not cut to a commercial. We were all gripped in a drama. We could not turn our heads or our hearts.

Until that moment, almost no one knew that this player, a popular young member of the Buffalo Bills, had founded a local charity in Buffalo to buy Christmas presents for that city's children. He had hoped to raise a few thousand dollars.

Two days after the heart attack and all the drama surrounding it, his charity took in more than $7 million, and the pledges were still coming in.

Some might call all these circumstances simply a coincidence—the timing, the impact, the heartbeat—a mere chaotic convergence of random events.

I look at it differently. A series of events, from tragedy to triumph, were brought together by prayer. This is an example of how we should view our lives, and even in moments of doubt, we must never forget that our faith has a purpose.

Chapter 17

Judge Not

"Do not judge, and you will not be judged. Do not condemn, and you will not be condemned. Forgive, and you will be forgiven."
—*Luke 6:37 NIV*

Judge not, that ye be not judged," from Matthew 7:1 (KJV), is a biblical truism most everyone knows by heart, if not by verse. Jesus spoke these words in the Sermon on the Mount, but it was a sentiment he shared on several occasions, such as in John 8:7 when he told a group preparing to stone a woman, "Let any one of you who is without sin be the first to throw a stone at her" (NIV). These messages are a small part of perhaps the most important sermon ever recorded. Jesus's words in the Sermon on the Mount, beginning in Matthew 5, contain the core benefits of historic Christianity. It is also here the Beatitudes appear and where Jesus first taught us the Lord's Prayer. But it is Matthew 7:1-3, however, that gets quoted most often by both pro- and anti-Christian groups. Christians use it to keep the faithful in line, while atheists use it like a cattle prod against those Christians who do sit in judgment, thus supposedly demonstrating the dark, intolerant underside of the religion.

But what does it mean, really? Before we begin, let's look again at the full quote:

> Do not judge, or you too will be judged. For in the same way you judge others, you will be judged, and with the measure you use, it will be measured to you. "Why do you look at the speck of sawdust in your brother's eye and pay no attention to the plank in your own eye? (Matthew 7:1-3 NIV).

I cannot read these lines without visualizing actor Jeffrey Hunter playing Jesus in *King of Kings*. I can still see him directing his comments directly at the assembled masses.

Likewise, in Luke 6:37, the author parrots Jesus, saying, "Do not judge, and you will not be judged. Do not condemn, and you will not be condemned. Forgive, and you will be forgiven" (NIV).

To be sure, on the issues of our modern day, such as abortion, premarital sex, homosexual behavior, crime, or drug use, we, as Christians, wish to have strong views consistent with what we prayerfully interpret as God's word. The trouble is we may interpret those words differently. We then search the Bible in vain for one verse after another to support our various opinions.

The Bible offers no absolute clarity about judging others' behavior. No clarity, that is, if we do not take Jesus's own words at face value. Once again, human imperfections seem to drive us toward making Matthew something more complicated than it needs to be. Unfortunately, this ambiguity leaves an imperfect humanity to interpret the meaning of his words.

I debated this subject with a pastor friend who toes a hard line on the subject. He said I was misinterpreting the verses in John, Matthew, and Luke and that Jesus's words were directed solely toward the hypocrisy of Pharisees, and we can indeed judge the actions of others. It was a position I found strange given that, in a modern-day sense, he would be a Pharisee.

At any rate, I found myself taking a contrarian view. Having read and reread Matthew and Luke, I believe that the straightforward interpretation is the best understanding. I believe Christ reminds us that our first duty is to put our own houses in order. If we wish to convince others of Jesus's righteousness, we must first live in the light of his goodness.

I think Jesus was both counseling and warning all of us who would follow him, saying we should not fall into the trap of thinking ourselves more righteous, godly, or special in our being than those others we would criticize.

I am reminded of what Isaiah wrote, specifically 55:7-9 (NIV):

> Let the wicked forsake their ways
> and the unrighteous their thoughts.
> Let them turn to the Lord, and he will have mercy on them,
> and to our God, for he will freely pardon.
> "For my thoughts are not your thoughts,
> neither are your ways my ways,"
> declares the Lord.
> "As the heavens are higher than the earth,
> so are my ways higher than your ways
> and my thoughts than your thoughts.

In short, I believe Jesus's words on judgment were intended to mean precisely what they sound like, rather than doing as many Christians today seek to do in redefining his words to suit our own perceptions and misconceptions. We must avoid the sin of pride and heightened self-righteousness in believing we have a right to arbitrarily opine about the faults of others.

We risk condemning ourselves when we judge those who fail to attain our own supposedly lofty goals. Specifically, we must avoid attempting to save souls by using the Bible as a cudgel, telling anyone who will listen—and even those who won't—what thou shalt not do.

It is for that reason I prayed over the verses in Matthew. As I did so, I was inspired to consider other verses credited directly to Jesus or his apostles.

I have sought the meaning of these words, and I feel that in some measure I understand what Jesus would say regarding his intent. He would not, in my opinion, be happy with the overly pious and sanctimonious language with which some modern Christians debate the concept of judging others.

Many Christians today assume we must never judge others lest we condemn ourselves. Others feel equally strongly in saying that as Christians, we must judge others and point out the error of their ways if only to save them from eternity in hell. Perhaps there is some truth in this, and the apostle Paul would undoubtedly agree. The difference today is that many Christians, if not most, would use the term "judgment" in the most pejorative sense. They would chastise others harshly, much as the Pharisees lorded over the Jews of the Old Testament.

Such Christians seem to claim for themselves the sole right to define what is right and wrong and damning to hell all those who disagree. They would pontificate with the same zeal as those a century ago who forbade dancing as a sin and who condemned a glass of wine as an instrument of Satan. Their philosophical descendants exist to this day, those who remind us on a regular basis that we must not, to save our own souls, violate what they have determined to be their rules.

In considering the question, it is essential to remember the context of any biblical references on judgment. Even Paul counseled on judgment in the early church communities as they grew in religious fellowship. He attempted to draw a fine line for Corinthians when he wrote, "What business is it of mine to judge those outside the church? Are you not to judge those inside? God will judge those outside. 'Expel the wicked person from among you'" (1 Corinthians 5:12-13 NIV).

Paul drew that line in his letters to the churches he helped establish. To him, there was a difference between those who were part of the body of Christ and those who were not. He felt those who had accepted Christ should hold themselves to a higher standard. He also warned of judging based on appearance and not on fact.

He counseled that there was a difference between holding people to account for purely criminal acts and passing judgment on who gets to enter the kingdom of God. The latter is certainly not our prerogative. It is the Lord's alone, and as has already been said, his ways are not our ways, nor his thoughts our thoughts.

For myself, I sense a middle course. In judgment, we should humbly seek to counsel and educate, not to condemn. We should seek to enlighten rather than judge, remembering that we will also be in the wrong at some point. To continue striving, with all due humility, toward a more perfect understanding of God's will in this world and the next.

God spoke to me as I prayed in quiet contemplation and laid out Christ's meaning behind his words.

"Think of it this way," God said to me. "Picture yourself looking out over a vast flooded plain. There is swiftly moving water everywhere. If anyone falls into the water, they risk becoming lost. They will be swept away if they do not get out. Now weaving through this plain is an elevated strip of land offering a solid path that provides people a safe way through the raging waters.

"The path is the way to eternal life in heaven. The waters are sin, which will sweep you to oblivion. All of mankind must risk traveling that route to eternity. Some manage to find their way through faith and grace, and many more do not. Then there are those who do not fall into the waters but rather jump willingly. They are left to struggle. They do not wish or choose to be saved.

"Your job, and those with you who hope to walk the path or even wade along the water's edge, is twofold. First, to assist those who wish to return to the path; you must extend a hand. Second, seek the aid of others to rescue yourself because you will also need their assistance.

"In short, you need one another to navigate the path successfully. This effort you should make with great humility and understanding. Your job is not to stand with dry feet on the shore and chastise those in the dark waters."

God's words lead finally and inevitably to the definition of our mission over the simple question of judgment. If Christians are to help and support one another, they must be able to advise and counsel one another honestly, and sometimes for their own good. They must also be able to receive counsel themselves.

You should not aim your counsel at those who do not wish it. This is where we fail. Jesus did not sit with sinners to remind them of their sins. He did not do this either by excusing their sins or threatening them with hell and damnation. Instead, he sought to help them find their better nature. No, Jesus did his work by showing them another way.

We, too, can bring people to Christ by showing them a better way, not shaming them over their failures. Rather, we should use his example and influence them by reflecting the light of Christ's goodness in our own lives.

Chapter 18

God 2.0

"And the people said unto Joshua, The Lord our God will we serve, and his voice will we obey."—Joshua 24:24 KJV

In the beginning, God created man. Now, man seeks to re-create God. The Lord wished for us to live without sin, but he knew we would not. He gave us free will, all the while knowing the result. Still, in our freedom to choose, we are not free.

No, we remain slaves, even if we do not realize it as such. We enslave ourselves, subservient to the worst within us—our desires, our hatreds, our weaknesses, and our lust. We attempt to pardon one another through the simple expedient of removing our transgressions from the list of God's sins as if that were within our power to do.

Yet what we do not grasp is that God's laws were not written by us but for us.

It is not for us to decide what is or is not a sin because we are imperfect beings. It is precisely because of our imperfections that we must not change God's decrees. It is easier to absolve ourselves than to change; this is precisely what we do.

God has asked me to warn mankind that it is not we alone who can cleanse ourselves of our many wrongdoings. He said we cannot simply wish them away or pretend they do not exist. He instructed me to tell you that I do not issue any judgment with my words but rather a caution to heed the will of God. Please do not ignore the truth simply because it seems easier for you in this life. Our existence now is nothing compared to what awaits us all, but our actions today affect our souls for eternity, not for the sins we have committed but for the repentance we have or have not shown.

Our churches—the institutions responsible for sharing God's words—have attempted to redefine what is sinful. They believe, with misguided sincerity, that they must keep their message relevant to today, to this day, and not to the days that have come before. These churches do not want to grasp that this day is no different than those hundreds and thousands of days that came before. In an attempt to speak to the people of this time, they have overturned two millennia of social norms in the name of moral inclusivity without regard to God's wishes. In the beginning, the Lord created man and woman. Now, some are pushing to raise the count from two genders to an infinite number, and you can be whatever gender you wish, depending on your mood at any given moment.

Collectively, humanity has also taken onto ourselves the prerogative of changing our gender, both literally and figuratively. God's will is not as sand—which shifts over time, adjusting to the currents flowing within men's minds—but as rock, firm and unchanging. This bedrock allows us to build a good foundation.

Today, churches operate under the premise that if you profess love for God and Jesus, nothing else matters. This piece is not about sinning. It is about acknowledging the existence of sin. Jesus did call on us to love, but he also tried to make us understand that love of God and choosing a lifestyle contrary to his wishes cannot go hand in hand.

He does not expect us to be perfect, but he does expect us to try to seek forgiveness when we fall short. Today, we act as if it is no longer relevant whether our lifestyles or choices contradict God's will. Instead, it is all about our parsing the definitions of his will. You don't want to be guilty of sinning? In today's world, it has become simple.

Just redefine the sin by negotiating it out of existence or by creating exceptions that accomplish the same effect.

Those who follow the teachings and the traditions of Christianity understand the call to love one another as Jesus and God love each of us. We all know the sentence that begins "judge not." However, that does not mean we must now blindly condone behavior contrary to God's commandments. We have all also heard the expression of hating the sin but loving the sinner. There is truth in that statement; still, there is a big difference between loving a sinner as part of our Christian faith and allowing the sinner to lead us down a slippery slope and away from salvation.

Many of today's churches are reinventing the Christian faith to conform to humanity's concerns. You cannot reinvent what is true in the hope of sounding more relevant. From the Bible, we know there is only one truth: Jesus. He did not come into the world to reinvent the word of God but to confirm and strengthen the word of God, and he said as much.

It is an inconvenient truth that God has presented humanity with the only possible roadmap to salvation. The way is narrow and winding. It is easy to lose one's footing, but finding one's way through salvation with faith in God and his help is possible. That is the only hope for Christians, who owe their salvation to Christ's sacrifice.

The Lord does not offer us the option of creating a substitute path to eternity using our own rules and our own sense of direction. As Jesus said, and as I have previously written, one must acknowledge the truth. That truth that Jesus speaks will set you free, but Jesus also said to go forth and sin no more. He died to forgive our sins, but he did not die to eliminate the concept of sin. In Matthew 5:17-18, Jesus says, "Do not think that I have come to abolish the Law or the Prophets; I have not come to abolish them but to fulfill them. For truly I tell you, until heaven and earth disappear, not the smallest letter, not the least stroke of a pen, will by any means disappear from the Law until everything is accomplished."

He came in fulfillment of scripture. He died to offer a way forward for all humanity. What vanity we must have to propose that, while believing in Christ and calling ourselves Christians, we believe we have the right to redefine what those terms mean.

Chapter 19

Why Is Having Faith so Hard?

"Everything is possible for one who believes."—Mark 9:23 NIV

Having faith is like dieting; it sounds simple until you get hungry.

It is one thing to talk about faith but quite another when it comes to execution. In truth, finding and maintaining faith is difficult. It is perhaps the most challenging aspect of Christianity. Not surprisingly, faith is also Christianity's most important aspect.

Sadly, the answer stares back at us in the mirror—we are our own worst enemies. Born with free will and endlessly distracted by the physical world around us, we are prone to get distracted by life's little sparklies rather than strive for any more profound meaning. Christ understood this about us.

As I've noted, I have not committed the Bible to memory. However, I pray for that ability. While I cannot cite the scriptures verbatim, I know the Bible well enough to paraphrase the verses, the parables, and "the words written in red," as many people do. Ultimately, I know the narrative, and perhaps that is more important. If one must choose, it is better to understand the message than just memorize the words.

In that vein, we know what the Bible says about the critical importance of faith, and the consequences of rejecting God's miracles.

In the Old Testament, after the Lord visited the ten plagues on Egypt, and freed the Jews from bondage, how long did it take to reject Moses? Those people had witnessed the parting of the Red Sea, yet how long did it take them to forget all that he had done?

Remember the parable about having faith the size of a mustard seed? Do you grasp the symbolism? These seeds are incredibly small. That is the point. Another time, Jesus talks to his disciples about their need to grow in their faith and resist doubts, yet how many miracles had they witnessed?

Matthew 8 relates the story of the Roman centurion asking Jesus to heal his servant. He tells Jesus he need not come to the centurion's house, which the soldier knew could have been socially difficult for Jesus. Instead, the soldier says that if he would merely say the word, the servant would be healed. In response, Jesus praises the man's faith.

Jesus even goes so far as to say that it is not through righteousness or good works one may attain heaven but through faith alone. The bottom line: You must believe, and you must have faith. If one has faith, the other things will come naturally from a newly altered view of what is essential in life, but it begins with that single word.

That sounds so good, doesn't it? And, as I said in the beginning, it sounds so straightforward—like saying, "I need to lose twenty pounds." You get so motivated and vow to lose those twenty pounds. Then you see this slice of apple pie an hour later—or a day later. Suddenly, your motivation goes down the drain, and at roughly the same speed as the pie goes in your mouth, you promise to begin again tomorrow.

Therein lies the problem and the struggle. We all need faith, but we are mortal and imperfect beings. We can never fully overcome the worries, doubts, and fears that control us. Fear and worry are the hallmarks of this plane of existence. They surround us and distract us because they are what is in front of us in our finite world.

Christ tells us what is required of us—but Jesus and heaven exist on a different level of existence, within a wholly spiritual realm. It is unseen and cannot be experienced in the normal sense by us. In this way, heaven is quite different from our physical world.

Still, despite what we all know of Christ's teachings, we will fall short. Faith is mentioned thirteen times in Matthew—and, yes, I googled that—and most were admonitions over having too little faith. We should not feel too bad, though. Jesus chastised his disciples many times for displaying too little faith, and they witnessed his miracles. Peter was the rock upon which Jesus would build his church, yet Peter denied Christ three times. The apostle Thomas refused to believe Jesus had risen until he had touched the crucifixion wounds, thus earning the name Doubting Thomas.

I recite all these examples because I, too, have times of doubt, of forgetfulness, of laziness. I have times when it seems much easier to absorb the distractions of this world and move my focus away from belief and faith.

It was during one such moment that God spoke to me and inspired me to share a new message. It was a concept I had not thought of before, yet upon reflection, it is not only obvious but imperative.

"Why do you have trouble believing in me?" he asked softly. It was not a rebuke but a serious question.

"What do you mean?" I replied.

I was confused. I certainly did believe in him. Despite that, I found myself worrying continually. I am no longer a young man and have limited resources to provide for my wife and myself as we age.

"You say you believe in me, and I have told you that you have no need to worry."

"Yes, of course I remember. I am a worrier. It gave me great comfort."

"And have not I proven time and again that you will be given what you need?"

"Well, yes."

"And did I not also say you would have other serious issues to face in your life, but that money would not be one of them?"

"Yes."

"And yet, you continue to worry."

"I can't help it. Living is expensive. I know what you have told me, but …"

"Have you thought about this: that belief and faith go hand in hand? If you believe in me, truly believe, then faith is mandatory. In the end, you cannot have true belief without faith. It is like a tree. Its trunk is belief, and its branches are faith. For the tree to thrive or even exist, it must be in unison—trunk and branches.

"If you believe, then you must have faith. If you have faith, then you believe in me and in what I tell you, and if this is so, you should not be troubled with your existence. Your faith will give you the strength to overcome your fears. It really is as simple as that. Of course, the reverse is also true. If you worry about things when I have told you not to, then your faith is weak, and that means you do not fully accept or believe in me."

Now, perhaps to others, this might seem an obvious train of thought, but until that moment, I had not put those two things together.

"Then what should I do, Lord, when these troubling thoughts come to me? I sometimes cannot help myself."

He replied, "Just repeat yourself, 'Have faith … have faith … have faith.' Think of it as a meditation, and your soul will be comforted."

And, of course, he was right.

Strengthening my faith brings peace through the most troubling and trying times. Now I more fully understand that his role for me, and my role for myself, is in God's greater glory, not my own.

If I can remember that, then I need never fear.

Chapter 20

The Easter Cross at Sunset

"You are the God who performs miracles; you display your power among the peoples."—Psalm 77:14 NIV

Miracles are funny things. Not funny in the humorous sense, but in the unusual and unexpected sense. We cannot predict them; we can only remember them. They sometimes appear in response to a plea for help. Other times, they appear spontaneously to remind us of God's presence and our place in his plan.

Easter 2020 was one such occurrence of the latter. My wife and I were hosting four other couples for a late-afternoon Easter cookout in our backyard. Our rental house was on the eastern shore of the St. John's River in Jacksonville, Florida.

Other than Easter, there was nothing particularly outstanding about this day. We had a huge outside table, salvaged from our last house, and it now sat in the massive backyard, affording us a tremendous view of the river and downtown. Despite the day, we had not gathered specifically for any religious significance; it was just a chance to gather friends together.

As the ten of us sat around the table, eating, laughing, and talking, the conversation turned to religion as it must on an Easter Sunday. We all politely danced around the subject, no one wanting to make any definitive statements for fear of isolation. We were all good, practicing, and politically correct Christians who wished to forgive everyone's transgressions while excusing any and all behavior. Two of the couples at the table were unmarried and living together, a situation that was once considered sinful but to which we paid no attention. No, why should we? We were all Christians, confidently forgiven, and sins be damned.

We thought ourselves a superior and thoughtful group of believers who knew all the rules but chose not to grasp the substance. The unspoken but universal truth was that the group felt it was more important to be universally inclusive than adhere to our shared faith's genuine tenets. We could not allow ourselves to condemn the acts of sinners if not the sins themselves. Doing so would have made them feel unwelcome or ashamed in today's language. Instead, we sat cheerfully pontificating about our enlightened spiritual beliefs like so many lemmings at the edge of a cliff.

Eventually, the conversation came around to God and miracles and how there aren't any miracles anymore—a politically correct line of thought on an Easter Sunday. The world seemed to have outgrown their need, or at least that was the table's consensus. As one, we proclaimed that Christianity had evolved past its more brutal past and into a more rational space where such ostentatious acts were merely too much show. After all, mankind had grown up. We all believed in Christ, and wasn't that enough?

Or was it?

As I've said before, the Bible says, "You will know the truth, and the truth will set you free" (John 8:32 NIV), but have we ever stopped to understand what that means truly? The truth of the Bible is Christ. The lone path to salvation is a belief in Christ, but to truly believe and love Christ, you must follow his path and teachings. It is pointless to continue saying you believe in Christ while making the conscious choice to continue in sin. You cannot love Christ and love sin. As Jesus says, you cannot serve two masters.

In short, we betrayed ourselves as fine Christian hypocrites.

Of course, this is merely an aside. We never discussed such matters so bluntly. I think we were all too embarrassed, afraid of exposing ourselves as "too Christian" or "too extreme" in our faith. Instead, we choose pseudononchalance, like someone smoking their first cigarette and pretending they'd been doing it for a lifetime.

We had set the stage. The city and the river were the backdrop. All the actors were in their place. The director was about to call the cue.

At this moment, I looked across the river toward the northwest. That section of Jacksonville was about three miles away, on the opposite side of the St. Johns River. I twisted around further and saw the brilliant red orb of the sun sitting just about the horizon.

Casually, I glanced at my watch and noted the time; it was 7:53. I noticed the time only because the cookout was going into its third hour. Then, I looked back to the northwest and was stunned by what I saw.

There, clearly visible on a building on that opposite shore, was the sign of the cross, glowing red in the setting sun's light.

I froze in silence. Had the building owners planned some unique light display, something that would not be uncommon in a southern city? It was the same blood red as the sunset, leaving no doubt about its origin.

Instantly, I pointed out the spectacle to the others at the table. None of the others had noticed it, and we all stared in awe. The table went silent. No one knew what to say. At first, someone suggested a simple light display until the cross vanished with the sun's setting. Finally, a few muffled voices expressed surprise, confusion, awe, and some barely concealed doubt that what had been visible had been visible.

The dinner party suddenly ended amid expressions of, "Look how late it is … Is it that late already?" Within fifteen minutes, everyone was gone.

I want to say I had no doubt what I had seen, and I would like to say I had witnessed a miracle, but to do so would be to give me too much credit. While the event captivated me, I was not wholly convinced.

Saying nothing more, I devised a simple test, and the next day, at the same time, I returned to the backyard, sat at the table, and waited for the sunset. It was in the same evening sky, and a red orb was setting on the horizon. Everything was the same … save one.

The cross did not appear. It should have, had it been a simple case of the light playing a trick, but the building was dark.

A glowing red cross appears on the side of a building at the setting sun on Easter Sunday. It is a simple, powerful, yet understated miracle.

Chapter 21

What Is Forever?

"The Lord gave and the Lord has taken away."—Job 1:21 NIV

For everyone, one particular moment always stays with them, one defining their existence. I have a vivid recollection of my moment in time. It was in the 1960s, and I was sitting in the car with my mother. I was eight years old then, and we were driving by our church—Rock Spring Presbyterian Church—but it was not a Sunday. It just happened to be on the way. I looked to my left and saw the beautiful dark beam and stucco building.

They built the church in 1922 in Gothic and Tudor Revival styles, but these are merely details. To a young boy, none of this mattered. It was a magnificent structure, entire of secret passageways, back stairs, and seemingly hidden rooms.

Each year at Christmas, we erected a live nativity scene, complete with a manger, Jesus in the form of a plastic doll, and real people as the wise men. In later years, I volunteered to be a shepherd. In my historical garb and false beard, I tended to three weary and bored sheep who slept through each evening's experience.

We had recently moved from our house to another across town, and I wondered what would become of our life in the church. All these thoughts went through my mind in a split second while we sat at the red light, and at that moment, I had an uncomfortable revelation.

"Mom," I said softly, "nothing lasts forever, does it?"

"No, Mark, it doesn't."

"We all die?"

"Yes." The response was matter-of-fact, emotionless, and delivered without any empathic understanding of a child of such an age asking such a question.

"What about buildings?"

"No. Nothing lasts forever. Not buildings, not people, nothing."

"Even if a building lasts a thousand years, it falls down someday?"

"Yes."

"Not even steel?"

"Not even steel."

I pressed myself back in my seat, terrified by the enormous implications of these few words. Nothing lasts forever—not buildings, not steel, and not me. That last part scared me most of all. I would not last forever? I had never given that a moment's thought.

Even today, six decades on, I don't know why she gave answers in single syllables. I have no idea whether she was distracted by her thoughts or did not care to carry on what might have seemed a morbid line of questioning.

Finally, the light changed, and we drove on. I looked back at the beautiful old building and wondered: If my church would not stand forever, what of me? What of my life? And I think of all the things she might have said that could have softened the blow to comfort a child coming face-to-face for the first time with the concept of their own mortality.

However, I do not blame her for failing to grasp my questions' meaning. Her answers were correct as far as it went. Nothing in this physical world lasts forever. Today, I know that even the earth's destruction will one day come, either in the final reckoning or when the sun goes nova.

Unfortunately, she missed a crucial opportunity to talk with me on a Christian level—some might call it a spiritual level—about the eternity that comes with belief in and love of God. He is eternal, and his love is eternal. Unlike bricks of clay and girders of steel, which will all one day decay, our souls will live forever in heaven with God and Jesus.

Perhaps that seems too metaphysical to some or too philosophical for an eight-year-old to understand, but it was still, to my mind, a missed opportunity. It would all be understood by any child, either on a shallow level or perhaps provide a deeper spiritual comfort, depending on that child's grasp. Either scenario would have been preferable to the alternative presented to me.

She did not offer up these thoughts, however, and I have spent the better part of a lifetime wondering over the subject and ultimately left to find my way to God.

Perhaps that is as he intended.

Chapter 22

Why Bad Things Happen

"God's ways are as mysterious as the pathway of the wind and as the manner in which a human spirit is infused into the little body of a baby while it is yet in its mother's womb."—Ecclesiastes 11:5 TLB

So many bad things occur in the world on a daily basis, and each time, people ask, "Why do these things happen? Why does God let them happen?" I have asked that question myself. None of us feel like we deserve it, and for most of us, that is probably true.

Perhaps the most ironic part of these circumstances is why we link God with tragedies that befall us. What people cannot, or will not, understand is that humanity makes its own path, sows its own seeds, and reaps its own harvest. We are like a global Rubik's cube with ten billion people interacting at any moment.

Understanding God's role in these moments in our lives requires a two-pronged understanding. First, as I said, it is we who are responsible for most of our troubles, and by "we," I mean mankind collectively. Everyone tearfully asks God. "Why did you let that happen?" The reality is if someone chooses to do something evil, that is their choice, not God's. The innocent victim must blame that someone, for that is where the blame lays. God did not perpetrate the evil or the accident, but he becomes everyone's go-to for blame.

This fact does not mean God does not answer prayers or perform miracles, for he most certainly does. What it does mean, and what we should constantly remember, is that God gave us free will. It was perhaps his greatest gift to us: the ability to decide for ourselves even in the face of his disapproval of our decision. However, he expects us to grasp the consequences of the world landscape we create for ourselves. If those consequences force you to reevaluate your life and accept the Lord and Jesus, then so much the better.

Second, despite our best attempts at bad behavior, God does talk to all of us. Sadly, surprisingly, few of us listen, and even fewer recognize his voice. That is the very nature of our existence.

God encourages us to take the proper path. Only when we attempt to listen and ask for his grace and guidance do we have any chance of happiness. God does not wish us to be unhappy; he does not desire to cause us pain. If we accept Jesus and believe in God, we will be saved. If we do not, then we will not.

We make that choice, and then we alone are responsible for the consequences.

CHAPTER 23

The Bible Is Infallible, Right?

"All Scripture is God-breathed and is useful for teaching, rebuking, correcting and training in righteousness."—2 Timothy 3:16 NIV

One question I have always had: Is the Bible the literal, infallible word of God? While being a Christian, at least philosophically, since childhood, I never understood the human desire to place the Bible in that lofty place. Infallible, really? Enlightened, I could understand, but infallible? Certainly, Jesus's words—the so-called words in red—are, I believe, genuinely the words of Christ, but I have known many good people over the years who hold as a central tenant of their faith that the entire Bible must be the perfect and undisputed word of God.

On this sentiment, they were unyielding, while I was equally adamant that their faith in that tenant, while admirable, was personally dangerous. To me, their entire belief system hinged on the notion of absolute perfection. It was like being balanced precariously on the point of a pin.

"If I find just one error in the Bible," I pointed out, "I cast your entire faith into doubt."

Needless to say, this line of reasoning did not endear me to any of them. Being good Christians, however, they only shook their collective heads politely and promised to pray for me. I welcomed the prayers but not the unspoken message within them.

As with so much of that which surrounds Christianity, there is a subtlety and duality that I believe humanity has difficulty comprehending. One must be a student of history, culture, and geography to understand the nuance of the word.

In my newfound closeness and prayerful dialogue with God, I dared pose that question to him. The answer I received was both surprising and obvious at the same time.

"The answer," God whispered to me, "is quite simply that the Bible is my word. It says as much in John 1:1: 'In the beginning was the Word, and the Word was with God, and the Word was God' (NIV). It is my message to humanity. It is a synthesis of where man has come from, where you are, and where you are going. The question, however, is not whether my words and thoughts are perfect. Instead, any perception of imperfection lay with those who read my word. My words—my thoughts—were put in a form that humanity could comprehend."

He continued, "Let me put it another way. I am infinite. My experience is eternal. I was here before the first stars lit the night sky. I was here before there was a here. Humanity's vision is the opposite; it is myopic. My vision, knowledge, and reach are all wholly beyond the range and scope of your understanding. You experience your short temporal lives in a literal, linear way. For you, there is a yesterday, a today, and a tomorrow. These concepts are meaningless to my existence. I could tell you that time is meaningless and that existence is not truly linear, but could you comprehend the full ramifications of that statement? I can tell you that, but you could not comprehend it. You are incapable of processing that experience. In the Bible, it is written that my people waited hundreds of years for me to bring them out of Egypt, but to me, it was less than the wink of an eye. Time, as you call it, is relative.

"True, I created you in my image, but on your level of existence, you are less than a shadowy reflection of me. I know some men have attempted to explain it, saying time is an artificial construct created by man, but can any of you define what that really means, or how you perceive it?

"Why do you think my son Jesus taught in parables? He had to do so because the fuller thoughts behind those parables are beyond your grasp, and even then, standing before his apostles, he had trouble making himself understood. Still, that was the only way to bring my concepts, desires, and plans to a level humanity could even begin to grasp. If I were to reveal to you all that I am and all that heaven is, you could not fathom the immensity of it. Mankind has never understood that words place limitations on the infinite, which is impossible. True existence is fully beyond your imagination. To be grasped, it must be experienced, but even if you did, could you write it down for others to comprehend? How can the finite begin to explain the infinite?"

"Then," I dared ask, "how is it that I can understand you?"

"I am communicating on your level of comprehension. I am only communicating to you that which you can grasp and in a manner you can comprehend."

I pondered the apparent truth of that comment. "But you are all powerful. Could you not just give us complete understanding? Couldn't you give us the perfect truth?"

"You forget, I gave you free will! Yes, I could give you absolute truth—or at least such truth as you could grasp at this level of existence—but even then, humanity would reject it. Knowledge and wisdom are not the same thing. Knowing is not the same thing as grasping the underlying meaning. Only by growing and learning can you hope to attain the wisdom I will not give you. You must earn wisdom. It is not something freely given on a whim. It would mean nothing to you.

"Is not my strategy clear? Your free will determines your path. From Eden onward, this is a journey of your own making. I knew it would be so, much as that fact saddens me. I wanted you to develop in your own way. You chose your path, not me. I only provided the signposts.

Now, I want mankind to grow as any father would wish his children to grow. If I were to tell you, rather than guide you, would you understand any better than your children understand you? How often do human parents say, 'Because I said so'?

"For instance, I know you have told your children that some people can only learn the hard way—painfully, through repeated mistakes. That has been mankind's choice. Now we are on the path of your choosing. I walk beside you to help those of you who have any measure of understanding to reach my goal. Yes, it is painful for mankind at times, but even through the pain, if you believe and have faith and find comfort in my love, you will achieve all that I desire for you.

"All I ask of you in return is that you love one another as I have loved you; to trust in the Lord, your God; to accept my word; and obey the commandments I have given you. Trust in your heart to know the truth. As my son said, 'Know the truth, and the truth will set you free.' Understand that he is the truth of which he spoke. Let yourself move past the shallow debate over mere words on a page and to the deeper meanings and guidance which resides beneath the surface."

"So," I said finally, defiantly, "you never answered my question. Is the Bible your infallible word or not?'

"I would answer it thus. Do you remember when we first talked, and you challenged me to provide you with an O-ring?

"Yes, of course," I replied sheepishly. "I was hoping you wouldn't."

"Seriously? No matter. Do you also remember when you discovered the O-ring was gone, what I said to you then?"

"Yes. You said that now you would teach me the meaning of faith."

"Then have faith then. The Bible is written as I wished it written. If humanity finds ambiguity in its passages, that is humanity's fault for failing to understand. When your mind turns to the Bible, study on it, pray on it, and try to understand the meaning of it, but do not question it. Instead, use it as you would any tool to bring yourself closer to me. It is perhaps the hardest lesson mankind must learn: to believe, and to have faith, always, no matter what comes. You must have faith. With it, you can move mountains or understand anything put before you. Not because I have willed it but because you have grown enough to begin to grasp it. Remember, faith is the key. That is the beginning and the end of everything."

"Faith?"

"Yes, haven't you wondered why everything regarding Jesus seems to have multiple possible answers? There are many examples. Consider Moses; he freed his people from bondage. They witnessed my miracles, and yet, in no time at all, they began making statues of idols. Or take Jesus and his shroud. It really is his burial shroud, but the final proof eludes you. He raised people from the dead, made the blind see and the crippled walk, and yet they still would not believe. Some ask if Jesus was even born. Was he a real person? Did he really speak those words written in red, as you call them?

"Humanity's memory is short. Even yours, though I do not condemn you for it. You witnessed a miracle, and yet still you struggle. Christianity comes down to one thing: Faith. For those who have true faith, all things are possible. For those who grasp it and believe, there are rewards in heaven."

Chapter 24

Find Your God Sense

"Truly I tell you, if you have faith as small as a mustard seed, you can say to this mountain, 'Move from here to there,' and it will move. Nothing will be impossible for you."
—Matthew 17:20 NIV

We all know the five senses that make up our existence. These senses define our world and our place in it. Oddly, while we need these senses to survive, they also get in our way of our relationship with God. To help fight that battle, I believe we would all work at developing our sixth sense: Our God sense.

In my other writings, I have speculated on the nature of our existence. I have compared our lives to the observations of light, with its waves and photons. Likewise, we observe the world around us with our five senses. We can only process with our eyes and ears or with what we can taste, smell, or touch. These senses operate on this level of existence, meaning that we can only perceive this level of existence. Perhaps this is why the ancient pagan religions appealed to humanity of the day. Those mythical figures were based solely on human senses. On the other hand, we know, through the life and teachings of Jesus Christ and the earlier Hebrew prophets, that there is another level, a higher level. A true God, the only God.

I have also written of the duality of our soul, which resides within but separate from the physical body we occupy. It is also influenced by the limits of five senses, and yet the quantum nature of our soul knows there is something more, something we cannot see, hear, taste, smell, or see. On some level we know that God exists, whether we want to believe in him or not.

To grow as Christians, we must develop that sixth sense that allows us to sense God is both within us and all around us. That is the God sense, but how do we do develop our awareness of God?

The simplest answer is prayer. That's the best way to start, but there should be more. A relationship with God is like any other relationship. It requires more than a one-way conversation. Of course, prayer is crucial, but you must also listen with your heart and with your mind. God will be answering you, or at least trying to talk to you.

Almost all people like to hear themselves talk more than anything else. For most of us, listening is not a mastered skill, hence the old saying that God gave us two ears and one mouth for a reason. This is our problem in accepting God's plan; we are not listening.

That is what changed for me—I began to listen. I get no credit for this fact. It was more a matter of God speaking so loudly that I could no longer avoid the conversation.

For most of my life I sensed the Lord's whispers, asking me to get about the work for which he had tasked me. It was so gentle I ignored it, much as one would the wind blowing through the trees. It was that subtle. It was only when I asked a question and opened my mind to hearing a reply that my world became different; that I became different.

How many times in my life had I not opened my mind, not waited for a reply? I had not bothered to listen because I had been too busy telling God what he could do for me, not asking what I could do for him—or for my fellow man.

He does speak to us. He talks to all of us, but we have free will. He gave us the power not to listen, but we do so at our own peril.

He does love us, and he wants the best for us, but if we reject him then that is our choice, and we must accept the consequences. So many people today believe that God's love will keep us safe from what might otherwise befall us, all the while rejecting him. His message to us is clear. Our portion is faithfulness to his teachings and his laws and to serve the Lord with devotion and love. This is the path to eternal life.

Those who believe they can do as they please, who redefine sin to suit their own desires and disregard the Lord's will, find a harsh judgment. This judgment is not one of his making but of their own. It was the path they chose. So many people speak thoughtlessly about a God that lets evil happen without comprehending that the evil comes from the interplay of Satan and the actions of humanity. Too often we act on our five senses and seek the sinful, the easy pleasure, or the corrupt path while paying lip service to God and Jesus.

Accepting them as your savior is much more than a trivial gesture or a casual thought. We cannot wish sin away by simply redefining what is sinful. His arms are wide open and welcoming, but you must make the commitment. You must accept Jesus as your savior and, in his words, go forth and sin no more (John 8:11).

We all know this is impossible, but we must try, and be willing to genuinely repent and seek forgiveness when we fail. It is important to make a sincere effort. God does not require that we be perfect, but he does want us to try and to be better than we are. We are not called to be better in order to reach God; rather, it is the reverse. In reaching for the Lord's forgiveness through Jesus, we find ourselves becoming better people.

This is where developing your God sense comes into play. We need to turn away from the temptations of the five senses of this mortal world and attempt to focus on that voice within us that calls out of Jesus.

As we accept Jesus, we begin to naturally turn away from the temptations of our human senses and become the better person we are seeking to become.

CHAPTER 25

Second Chances

"If we confess our sins, he is faithful and just to forgive us our sins and purify us from all unrighteousness."—1 John 1:9 NIV

The dream frightened me. Its message troubled me even more. But, I wondered, was it merely a dream? I didn't believe that. I am sure it was not. It was God who had spoken, and the vision terrified me.

Only days before, on Thanksgiving Day, I felt completely at peace. It was the first time in three years I could say that. The Lord had spoken to me three years ago, in the midst of my despair, simply telling me to have faith in him and not worry. I will never forget the night he spoke to me. I should add that this was not the first time we had spoken, but it was the first time I'd thrown myself entirely at his feet in willing submission to his will. I was distraught and broken to the bottom of my soul.

"Have no fear," he told me. "I know you worry about providing for your family, but I tell you, you do not need to worry. You will face other challenges, but you need not worry about that."

True to his word, things worked out as he had promised, and as they improved, I found myself slipping back into my easy ways. It was not a matter of being overtly sinful, but I found myself engaging less with God and more re-engaging not with God's desires for me in this world but my own, and even as I did so, I sensed there would come a day of reckoning.

That day came last night.

"You have become too comfortable," I heard his voice say. "I can see I may have been too generous with you."

"What?" I jerked awake. Had I been dreaming? Was I still?

"God?" I mumbled, still unsure if I'd been imagining the words. "What's wrong?"

"You," he said. "You are not keeping your word to me. You made a commitment to me; we had a covenant. I have kept my word. What have you done? You promised to glorify my name, to share the joy of your salvation with others. Neither of these things have you even tried to accomplish. If you do not keep to your word, why should I?"

Those words terrified me. The past years had been hell, figuratively if not literally. It was not an existence I cared to repeat.

Finally, exhausted and with no end in sight, I wished merely to be put out of my misery. In my despair, I'd called on God, not truly expecting or, frankly, believing I was worthy of salvation. I had been wrong, very wrong.

As I said, surprisingly—or perhaps not—he answered my prayers, and in the process, I began a journey of self-discovery. I saw the many things I'd done wrong, both recently and throughout my life. It was not a pretty sight, but one I had to face. It was a thought journey made easier by God's forgiveness.

I knew God, through Christ, had forgiven me all those wrongs, but still, they must be reviewed and understood, not to punish myself but to learn from my mistakes. But as the storm had begun to ease, I once again became preoccupied with the comforts of this world. Time and again, I found myself shifting my focus onto this existence. In part, I suppose I did so because, as a mortal being, this place was at the core of my human existence. I spoke with God less and less and did not seek his advice and guidance.

"This was not what angered me," he said, snapping me out of these thoughts.

"God, I am not resisting or ignoring you," I pleaded. "I just do not know how I am to serve you. I am waiting for you to give me a sign."

This statement was not entirely true. I had been lazy, preoccupied, distracted, and other things. I wasn't fooling anyone, not me and certainly not God.

"You have not heeded my call for you to use those gifts I have given you to honor and glorify me, to tell others about how you have been saved by grace and how they may also be saved. That is the promise you have broken."

"But I do believe in you. I believe in your son, Jesus Christ. I believe in the promise of eternal life through his sacrifice."

"Belief is not enough. You must be active in your faith. Remember, Satan believes in my existence also. I expect more of you."

My next thought was, at the same time, subservient, apologetic, self-centered, and wrongly directed.

"No, God, please," I muttered. "Please. I cannot go back to the hell I went through. Please do not abandon me."

Even as I gave voice to that line of argument, I realized the weakness of it, a point he reminded me of at once.

"Why are you afraid? Is it because of what you might lose belonging in this world or your salvation in the next? A thought for you: What you may feel is at risk in this world is nothing compared to what you risk for all eternity."

"Lord," I whispered, "forgive me. I am only human, and I live in this world. This existence is all I know. I also know this: The past three years have been hell on earth, at least to me. I have no desire to go through an eternity of it."

"I understand," God said evenly. "So I say to you again, will you use the gifts given you in my name? Will you use that voice to help save others?"

"Yes, Lord, but will they listen?"

"That much you can leave to me and them. The final choice will be theirs, just as it is with you."

"I choose you, Lord."

"I know."

This conversation may not be an original thought, and I have no proof that the voice I heard or the conversation I had was nothing more than a dream. I know that, but I choose to believe the experience was real. Not just real to me, but absolutely, objectively real.

I also know that honoring God and his call is a process. It can happen in an instant, but it rarely does. While the moment of true salvation may seem like an epiphany, that pot has probably been simmering for some time, but only in the final moment, when you taste it, do you realize it is ready.

So it is with the Lord. We plant the seeds in our youth, but we harvest the crop when the tree is mature and ready to bear fruit.

Chapter 26

Dichotomy

"The world and its desires pass away, but whoever does the will of God lives forever."—1 John 2:17 NIV

"How can the meek inherit the earth," I asked God many times as a child, "or the poor in spirit inherit the kingdom of heaven?" I do not know if he ever answered. I did not bother to listen. For many decades, I refused to hear him. His voice fell on deaf ears. I heard only my own words, and my mind remained closed. I certainly did not consult any books on the subject. In truth, there were questions, but the questions did not bring forth the necessary intellectual curiosity to ferret out the answer.

Was I honestly searching for the truth? No. Still, if only rhetorically, my questions continued. How can those who are first be last, or those who are last become first?

"Mark," God chastised me recently. "Now that you acknowledge me, it is time you understand the meaning of Jesus's words. They do not represent dichotomies, as you call them. No, they are a road map. They tell you where you are, where you should be, and what is at the end of your journey. Is that not what maps do?"

"Yes, Lord," I replied. "That is what maps do, but the beatitudes are not a map. They speak in riddles. Why?"

"Good, finally. Questions are good when one genuinely seeks the truth. They admit two things. First, one must be humble enough to know that one does not know everything. Two, when one is ready to listen, they admit they are open to learning what they do not know. Now, are you ready? You have not been for far too long. Since you were a child, you have questioned, and yet you have not sought the truth. Now, you are ready."

"Yes, Lord, I am ready. I believe I am."

"Good. So why do you think this is an opposition, that the meek will inherit the earth? Do you think that warriors will inherit the earth? That fighters will conquer everything their eyes can see, and what of competing warriors? Will there eventually be one who conquers all? No, I say to you that all the conquerors and the warriors will one day destroy one another and all that surrounds them. And what if someone did conquer everything? What would they have won? Everything in your lives is fleeting. My realm is eternal, and only those who are humble may inherit my kingdom and live with me in heaven. Only those who do not crave power and glory may attain salvation because they truly understand such power and glory is not my purpose. The world and heaven are more than you can comprehend. Until the day comes when mankind can grasp this, you must have faith."

"But what about the other beatitudes?"

"They are self-explanatory to you, at least to some degree. When Jesus said blessed are those who mourn, he meant those who mourn more than just loss in the human sense. He was not speaking of losing a loved one. My son was talking about mourning the loss of innocence, the loss of self to sin, and even losing your way because of sin. So it is not just loss in a physical way, but more importantly, loss in a spiritual way as well."

"And the poor in spirit? That sounds to me like they are unsure of their faith."

"Let's turn this one on its head. Another word for poor might be unworthy. Would it make more sense if Jesus had said, 'Blessed are those who, despite their faith, feel unworthy of salvation'? So many in this world feel so sure of their attaining eternal life that they are unable or unwilling to see their own shortcomings. They simply presume, and that bothers me."

"But aren't they just secure in their faith? Why is that wrong?"

"It depends on their humility. There are two types of people: those whose faith leads them to be humble, and those whose presumption distracts them with arrogant self-importance. Those who are sincerely humble grasp the true meaning of faith. There is a difference between righteous and self-righteous. Now do you understand?"

As I absorbed God's words, I saw my error. Instead of a dichotomy, the beatitudes serve as a path to the Christian faith. They both articulate a course for living and encapsulate the fundamental teachings of Jesus, but in doing so, I have come to see that they also set out the differences between mankind and God. They highlight the differences between the moral and the eternal and contrast heaven and earth. In short, they try to express to imperfect man how to attain the kingdom of God. Simply stated in 1 John 2:17, "The world and its desires pass away, but whoever does the will of God lives forever" (NIV).

This verse is a theme that runs throughout the Christian faith. I was not entirely wrong, however. Jesus was trying to make mankind see that our approach to living was precisely the opposite of what it should be to attain God's kingdom. Consider Jesus's miracles: forgiving the adulterer, turning water into wine, and restoring the insane to sanity, to name a few. The effort to draw a clear distinction seems obvious.

But the symbolism goes far beyond Christ's words. The entire Christian faith and God's many works seem to use this same sense of opposites. Perhaps this is nowhere more evident than Christ's death on the cross. His crucifixion was a punishment reserved for the lowest of the low: traitors, murderers, and the worst criminals.

It was the most gruesome spectacle Rome could devise, reserved, in Rome's opinion, for those who deserved nothing less than a horrid and tortured death. And yet, in his infinite wisdom, God turned this terrible symbol into the greatest victory that mankind could witness. From the lowly and humiliating execution on the cross sprang a faith that is followed today by billions worldwide.

God seizes eternal life from death. He makes the lame walk and makes well the sick. In all these things, he shows the difference between his eternal will and our world. He shows us the way by providing a path to salvation for the unworthy human race.

We would do well to listen, just as I have finally begun to do. Granted, it took me a few decades, but God can be patient.

Chapter 27

Be Careful What You Pray For

"If you believe, you will receive whatever you ask for in prayer."
—*Matthew 21:22 NIV*

We are all souls searching for meaning, wandering in a world we do not truly understand. We cast about in spiritual blindness, feeling our way through life. We grasp only the barest part of that which is around us and try to comprehend what we see, but we find only mere reflections, such as we might see in the water and the ripples that travel this way and that.

I did not say we were lost souls, for saying "lost" would imply we had once been where we ought but strayed off the path. No, we are not lost, because we have never been where we should have been. We all search in vain, trying to make our own way to salvation, knowing it is here, somewhere, but we are unable to see it.

That is why God sent his Son. He came as the beacon of light meant to guide us. We must follow him and hear his words. He brings illumination to our own meager, flickering torches—for those who believe in him will serve as a beacon to others. We are to be his reflections, the enlightenment of his word who will help those who come after us. We receive no credit for this; it is not an action of our own doing, no more than a mirror is the true source of light. The mirror, like ourselves, only serves to show the light of Jesus, who came to show us the way.

For us, the world is like a game of Mahjong Solitaire. The events of our lives are scattered with chaotic randomness. Our existence becomes focused on doing nothing more than matching up these pairs. Their assignment is random, and we see our task as finishing the game. We become myopic. Like life, we do not know what effect comes from removing each pair. Will it lead to the next move, or will that move be our last? We have no way of knowing if we are left to our own devices, and so, for our relationship with God, we have only prayer.

What is the nature of prayer? Of course, we pray when we are distressed or in need. Our desire and need for prayer is a direct correlation to our mental state. The sadder we are, the more troubled we are, the more we turn to prayer. When our lives seem full, it is our nature that prayer slips by the wayside. It seems strange, doesn't it, that we seldom say prayers or give thanks when things go well. We are walking the same path, and nothing can be changed except our current situation.

I know that most would say, "That is not true. I pray every day." I have no doubt that what you might say is, in fact, true. But ask yourself: Do you eat more when you are hungry or when you are full? Of course, we are all free—indeed, encouraged—to pray in our darkest times, and Christ himself says, "Ask and it will be given to you; seek and you will find; knock and the door will be opened to you" (Matthew 7:7 NIV). So praying in such times is not wrong. At other times, we show gratitude to God and Christ for blessings bestowed upon us. But giving thanks, while worthwhile, is only the beginning.

The apostles asked Jesus how they should pray, and he responded with the Lord's Prayer. In reading his words, you will see that first—and most important—we honor the Lord. Jesus then calls on us to accept God's will, to glorify his name, and to be subservient to his will. We need not seek any more than our daily needs, not our wants and desires. We ask for his forgiveness, as we promise to forgive others. Finally, we implore God to turn us away from our temptations and deliver us from evil.

Apart from the Lord's Prayer, what do you pray for? The truth is there is no set of rules, no specific guidelines for how we talk to God. Do we seek worldly things? Do we ask for grace? Certainly, we can pray for our friends, we can pray for understanding, or like the Miss America contestants, we can pray for world peace.

We should all give thanks for the blessings we receive, even if there are times when we do not understand the full extent of their worth. True prayer is more, however. When we pray, we should give thanks not only for what gifts we may receive, but more importantly, get below the shallow human tendency to rattle off a quick prayer without giving it serious thought. We must open our hearts to God, seek guidance, seek forgiveness, and seek his wisdom. Through thoughtful prayer we can learn of his plans for us and how we can best serve him.

Prayer can be the beginning of a conversation with the living God. It is not just speaking but listening as well. Learning this, and pursuing his guidance with an open heart, is the beginning of wisdom.

Chapter 28

The Joke Is on Us

"For the wages of sin is death, but the gift of God is eternal life in Christ Jesus our Lord."—Romans 6:23 NIV

I remember a joke from years ago that goes like this;
A wealthy man says to his wife, "Honey, if I lost all my money, would you still love me?"

Without hesitation, the wife replies, "Darling, of course I'd still love you." Then she adds, "I'd miss you, but I'd still love you."

I think of God whenever I think about that joke. You might think that's strange—why God?

My thought makes sense if you substitute a couple of words, like this:

"God, would you still love me if I broke all your rules and never sought repentance?"

To which God's reply would be, "Of course, my child, I would still love you. I would miss you in heaven, but I would still love you."

Hopefully, the message is clear. I am afraid so many modern Christians take the concept of God's unconditional love the wrong way. These Christians believe that acknowledging God and accepting his love is enough, that no further action is required. In a sense they are correct. The Bible does say that faith alone is the path to heaven.

However, they miss the incongruity of faith in God while reveling in sin. True faith in God should bring with it a desire to be better and to do better, and when we fail, we must humbly ask for forgiveness. Many modern Christians dismiss the need for anything further simply because God's love is infinite, which in their minds minimizes the need for soul-searching and seeking forgiveness.

God's infinite love, however, does not absolve us of all responsibility. Although human cultures and standards change, God's laws are unchanging.

Yes, his love is unconditional and without limit, but there is a difference between love and forgiveness. When you were a child, hopefully your parents loved you. They might have gotten angry and punished you, but their love was presumably constant. They might forgive you, yet even so, they might still be angry. Their forgiveness will hinge on you—have you acknowledged your wrongdoing and apologized? Have you asked for their forgiveness? And, having sought and received their forgiveness, have you gone back and transgressed again?

It is one thing to sin and, after seeking forgiveness, be forgiven. But when you repeat the sinful act, is forgiveness so easily obtained the second time or the third? Human parents have little patience for children who apologize only to reoffend.

But God has infinite patience. In fact, he requires only that you believe in him, accept the forgiveness provided through Jesus Christ, and each and every day attempt to live as God and Jesus would have you live.

God recognizes we are not perfect, and he realizes we will have failures. All he asks is that we trust and believe—to have faith. When we do this, he will work through us to bring about his will. The true bottom line is that his will is accomplished whether we wish it or not. He would rather we follow him, trust him, and allow him to bring about his plan, but through his infinite power, his plan will be achieved regardless of our individual choices.

When the Persian emperor Cyrus II, also known as Cyrus the

Great, conquered the Neo-Babylonian Empire, he allowed the Jews to return home to rebuild the temple. That time, God worked through Daniel, who told Cyrus about Isaiah's prophecies concerning the emperor and that he, Cyrus, had been chosen by God to restore his people. While a pagan, Cyrus believed Isaiah's words and acknowledged God, and God's will was done.

This short history lesson highlights the fact that God works through everyone, not just believers. Everyone.

Personally, I need look no further than myself to see the truth of these words. I have been saved and given new life, not for anything that I might have done, but to proclaim the truth and beauty of God's plan as well as the sacrifice of his son, Jesus Christ.

The bottom line is that God loves us now and forever. His love is eternal and infinite. It is not God who rejects us, but we who reject him. As God, he sets the rules and guidance for our existence. It is his right to define what is a sin. Sometimes he explains why something is a sin, and other times no explanation is needed because the reason is obvious and self-evident.

In Matthew 6, Jesus reminded us that treasures on earth are subject to destruction, while in heaven they are incorruptible:

> Do not store up for yourselves treasures on earth, where moths and vermin destroy, and where thieves break in and steal. But store up for yourselves treasures in heaven, where moths and vermin do not destroy, and where thieves do not break in and steal. For where your treasure is, there your heart will be also (Matthew 6:19-21 NIV).

The concept is simple. Heaven is infinite. Earth is finite. On earth, everything eventually dies and decays; it returns to its fundamental elements. Man is likewise two distinct things—the soul, which longs for God, and a physical form, which is of the earth. Our mortal part, our "adulterated nature," longs for this level of existence. It is this longing for the finite world that deceives us. This desire manifests itself as sin. Indeed, in and of itself, the desire is sin.

In any event, it is not his lack of love but our own choices—whether brought about through arrogance, indifference, or outright defiance—that block the path to our own salvation. To quote Pogo, a comic character from generations past, "We have met the enemy, and it is us."

As Christians we can do no better than to attempt to emulate God's eternal love, patience, and forgiveness. This can prove challenging because too often we are judged by others as being judgmental ourselves. Many people, especially nonbelievers, think we revel in our supposed superiority over the weakness of others. We cannot afford the luxury of living down to that reputation or expectation. Still, at the same time, we must speak the truth of God's divine plan for humanity. We must follow God's and Jesus's instructions and love our enemies, pray for those who wish us ill, and not judge those who do not believe as we do. We are not here either to preach to the choir or to chastise the peanut gallery. We exist to love, honor, and follow God. That is where our treasure is and where our heart should be also.

So to those of you who choose not to honor God but reject him because his rules are too hard, or because they do not fit with your personal choices, or because they are inconvenient, or because they are outdated and irrelevant in today's culture, please understand that your choice is your decision, not his.

Yes, he does still love you, regardless. He will miss you, but he will still love you.

CHAPTER 29

What Is Proof?

"Even after Jesus had performed so many signs in their presence, they still would not believe in him."— John 12:37 NIV

While wasting my time on social media one afternoon, a post caught my eye. It was an article written for a Christian website extolling the behavior of Jesus's apostles as evidence of Christ's existence. His reasoning was that only those who witnessed Christ's miracles and ministry firsthand would have been willing to lay down their lives as martyrs, and according to accounts, they were all martyred. Their deaths were gruesome. Some were beheaded, while others were crucified, scourged, or worse.

While I agree with the historical aspects of the article, I disagree with the conclusion. Several thoughts crossed my mind: the apostle Paul never met Christ, at least not in the flesh, and yet he, too, was martyred. His works also make up the bulk of the New Testament. It would seem he was as dedicated to the cause as the other apostles despite not having direct contact with the living Christ.

On a broader level, I became curious about the continuing efforts of my fellow Christians to wrap themselves up in the search for evidence. What evidence do they hope to find, and what do they hope it will prove?

If—and I do not doubt their word on this—they are Christians, then it would seem a pointless quest. To what end did they search and write? If they are people of faith, then they should need no proof.

If they seek to provide evidence to the nonbelievers, then they should know they are most probably wasting their time. We all know the old axiom, "If you believe, no proof is required, and if you don't, no proof is enough." So again, I ask: Why do they seem so committed to preaching to the choir?

I prayed on this topic and asked God for guidance. Not surprisingly, he responded, although not in the way I had expected.

"You are troubled," he whispered to me. "Why do you concern yourself with this subject?"

"Lord, I do not understand why these people keep searching for proof of your existence and of Jesus's existence. What are they trying to prove? Who are they trying to convince?"

"I call on all of you to come to me," he said softly, "and also to bring other people to me. Each person comes with their own strengths … and weaknesses. I would love for all of you to have perfect faith, but I know that is not the case."

"But why are they trying to prove that which should be accepted on faith?"

"If their inquiries and statement of proof bring one more person toward God, that is a good thing. Not everyone has the ability, faith, or confidence to simply accept me on face value."

"But—"

"Listen, have you not noticed that every mystery, every question, and every answer requires faith in the end? Jesus's burial shroud, for one. Clearly, it is real, yet there are those who are confident they can come up with a plausible human explanation. It was the same with the children at Fatima, the miracles at Lourdes, the plagues of Egypt, and the parting of the Red Sea; I could go on and on. Even after bringing my people out bondage in Egypt, they still doubted me. Humanity's memory is short, and you have an unfailing ability to ignore what is before their eyes."

"Not me, Lord."

"Yes, and it only took you fifty years to truly accept me. Be honest."

I said nothing. What was there to say?

"The point is that proof will always be in the eye of the beholder. These moments, like the Red Sea, will be accepted and remembered by those of faith. Others—even those who witnessed it—will disregard and deny that which happens in front of their own eyes."

It was then I understood—just as when Thomas doubted Jesus had risen, and Christ told him to touch his wounds.

To Thomas, Jesus said, "Because you have seen me, you have believed; blessed are those who have not seen and yet have believed" (John 20:29 NIV).

So I say to all of you: Blessed is he who has faith and believes.

Chapter 30

Endgame

*When they reached the place God had told him about,
Abraham built an altar there and arranged the wood on it.
He bound his son Isaac and laid him on the altar,
on top of the wood. Then he reached out his hand
and took the knife to slay his son. But the angel of the Lord
called out to him from heaven, "Abraham! Abraham!"
"Here I am," he replied.
"Do not lay a hand on the boy," he said.
"Do not do anything to him.
Now I know that you fear God, because
you have not withheld from me your son, your only son."
—Genesis 22:9-12 NIV*

God's voice came to me out of nowhere and without preamble or introduction. It was something I had gotten used to after so many conversations.

"I have spoken to you," he began, "about how precious your time is and your need to begin your testimony."

God's tone seemed stern.

"I have been working on my writing, as you instructed. I think it is going well."

"Of course, I know you have, but it is time to tell you something. You should know your life on earth is coming to an end."

"What?" I was too shocked to say anything else.

"You will write about this conversation. You will document my words so that those who read your writings will know that I have brought my words to you."

"But how will my death help document anything?" I paused a moment. "How will I die?"

"You have cancer, as you will soon find out. Now I wish you to write down these words and put them aside. Send them to yourself so you will have a date that predates your eventual diagnosis. In this way, other people will know our talks are genuine."

"… Very well," I responded after some hesitance. I was numb but acknowledged him obediently.

"And one last thing. You are to tell no one."

"But my wife—"

"You are to tell no one," he repeated. "I have a purpose in this. I will provide for your wife."

So I did as he said, although I had no reason to suspect anything was wrong. I felt fine, and I had no notable issues. Despite my earlier conversations, I first thought I had imagined this particular event.

That would change in a few months.

After a while, God's message propelled me to action, and I went to the Mayo Clinic for a routine checkup. They found nothing they deemed suspicious, so I told them what to look for, and when they took a second look, there it was.

They ran one test.

Then they said, "Maybe we should do another."

Then they said, "Perhaps we should do an MRI, but we're not too worried."

They must have been suspicious, however, because a biopsy followed that.

That last test confirmed what God had prepared me to hear.

How I finally received the news was funny. Not funny in the humorous sense—more in the odd sense, strange. I received an anonymous lab text with the test results on the Mayo Patient Portal.

No human interaction. No sympathetic voice. Just some words on the screen. After a week, I still had not spoken to anyone. Just more texts—texts on appointments, procedures, and checklists in preparation for procedures. Not one syllable of human compassion. That is big medicine in the twenty-first century, and perhaps a thought for another day.

Machines that scan you, texts that inform you, and robots that treat you; there is no humanity. Doctors seem to have become tangential to what should be the most humane part of the process.

The text was full of polysyllabic words signifying nothing, all except one: Cancer.

The news spun around in my mind, yet I did not cry, shake, or shout. Instead, thanks to God's warning, I felt a strange sense of peace. An unexpected calmness came over me. There had been times in my life when I wanted to move beyond this realm and return to heaven, but the thought of suicide was repugnant to me. I don't know; perhaps I was just too scared to do it to myself. Now, with cancer, maybe I didn't have to do anything. I could let a mass of random, unthinking cells grow out of control and handle that issue for me, but now that was not the path I wished to take.

God once told me I put no value on his gift of life, and he was right. Now, having found a reason for living, I was going to die. The irony was palatable.

When I thought of the warning God had spoken to me, I began to wonder. I saw that God was right—there is more to life than money. This fact has been mentioned in my writings many times, so I need not recount it again, but I did not expect this particular result or any result so quickly. I had hoped for a moment to breathe, but no.

The doctors eventually spoke with me. Their attitude was professional and indifferent, perhaps even dismissive. They gave me four treatment options: surgery, chemo, radiation, or do nothing. I learned I had a slow-growing cancer that could be treated or ignored in the short term. Doing nothing was hardly a comforting treatment plan.

The hardest part of this episode was not speaking to anyone, especially my wife, about what God had told me. She knew I had cancer, but she did not know all that God had told me long beforehand. There were other issues in my life that needed resolution before I could get treatment, so I delayed surgery for a time. I awaited that date with benign resignation. It sounds strange, but I was not troubled. Instead, I was blessed to be at peace with God's will.

Then God, in his mercy, spoke to me once again as I was about to have surgery.

"You have kept your word to me. You have told no one about my words to you," he said softly. "You have proved your faith and obedience; I will not let you die. It is not yet your time."

"Excuse me?"

"I challenged Abraham to show his faith and unquestioning obedience by telling him to sacrifice his only son, just as I would later do with my own son Jesus. Just as I tested Abraham with Isaac, so have I tested you. I needed you to see that your faith had grown. It was important you trusted in my word and proved yourself."

"But you cannot compare me to such an important person. I am certainly not Abraham. I am not worthy."

"I did not say you were Abraham, but all who believe in me will face times of testing, each according to my plan."

And now, as Paul Harvey would say, I'll tell you the rest of the story. It turned out the cancer was at a later stage than all the MRIs and biopsies had shown, but the doctor is convinced that he entirely removed it.

Now I wait and wonder. I know I will not die of cancer, at least not now. Though I know I will die of something someday, I am no longer afraid for God is with me always.

CHAPTER 31

One Final Thought

"Do not let your hearts be troubled. You believe in God; believe also in me."—John 14:1 NIV

I believe.
   Not because I can prove it, but because I cannot. I believe there must be something greater than ourselves, that this world is more than a conglomeration of plants and animals evolved by the whim of unthinking bits of DNA, and that we are more than random cells interacting merely through chance. There must be more to this plane of existence than mere chaotic convergence.

I do not need to understand it, I am not required to comprehend it, and God does not ask that I be able to explain it. I only need to accept it, and in so doing, I must humble myself in the acknowledgment that the world and God's plan are beyond my limited understanding.

It is not my place to understand God's plan, but just to accept that there is a plan. It is pointless for mankind to claim the right to even question the workings of an infinite God within the narrow understanding that restricts and confines of our finite beings.

In the end, we are left merely with faith and humility: to accept in the absence of explanation and to acknowledge we walk a path that, by design, is beyond our ability to comprehend.

For myself, I can only say this: I believe.

About the Author

Mark Barnette has had a variety of careers, from award-winning journalist to international educator and founding president of The American University in Dubai. Along the way, he served in the United States Air Force and also partnered in a production company that made several documentaries in collaboration with the BBC. In addition, he was executive producer and writer of the award-winning *John Ehrlichman: In the Eye of the Storm*, hosted by Tom Clancy.

www.ingramcontent.com/pod-product-compliance
Lightning Source LLC
Chambersburg PA
CBHW070204100426
42743CB00013B/3036